Changing Lanes

A CHRONICLE OF ONE YOUNG WIDOW'S
JOURNEY TO MAKE SENSE OF HER LIFE
FOLLOWING HER HUSBAND'S SUDDEN DEATH

STEPHANIE COOPER WILLOUGHBY

CHANGING LANES
By Stephanie Cooper Willoughby

Ì hope you enjoy this book!

Published by:
BOLD Company Books
www.theboldco.com

ISBN# 978-0692435298

You can connect with Stephanie online at:
www.livenowlivebold.com
facebook.com/scooperwilloughbyauthor
twitter.com/livenowlivebold

Table of Contents

Introduction 1

Year 1 {or that year some really crazy shit went down}.....3

1. Gotta Start Somewhere 13
2. I Miss You 18
3. Mindful of One's Matters 20
4. Dream a Little Dream 22
5. Tomorrow, You're Only a Day Away 25
6. Memories Fade, but the Scars Still Linger 26
7. Confidence in High Speed 30
8. Anger is an Energy 33
9. My Baby She Sent Me a Letter 37

Year 2 {or that year I tried to hide... until I realized I couldn't}.....41

10. With Liberty and Justice For All... Whatever 49
11. Ready, Set... Hang On a Sec 51
12. Bah Humbug 54
13. Happy Birthday Ethan 56
14. From the Mouths of Babes 58
15. More Genius from the Progeny 60
16. With Ten Miles Behind Me, and Ten Thousand More to Go 61
17. O'Tannenbaum, O'Tannenbaum 63
18. All's I Got is Time. Got No Meaning, Just a Rhyme 66
19. December Will Be Magic Again 68
20. My Eyes Are Green, 'Cause I Eat a Lot of Vegetables 70
21. Turn the Clock to Zero, Mack 73

Year 3 {or the year I decided I was tired of getting knocked around by grief}.....75

22. I Grab My Keys and a Beer 85
23. Now You're Stuck in a Moment, and You Can't Get Out of it 87
24. A Few More Words From the Mouths of Babes 90
25. Runnin' Down the Road Trying to Loosen My Load 92
26. Emancipate Yourself From Mental Slavery 95
27. Words Like Violence, Break the Silence 99
28. He Guided Me to Tennessee 103

29. There's No Other Pill to Take, So Swallow the One That Made You Ill.....104

30. Another Birthday 106

31. I'm Dreaming of a White Christmas 108

32. Baby it's Cold Outside 111

Year 4 {or that year the fog finally lifted... but then the dang water rose}.....117

33. I Wanna Talk About Mii 125

34. Tell it Like it is I (Valentine's Day Edition) 128

35. Do You Know What Today is? 129

36. Tell it Like it is II 132

37. Tell it Like it is III 133

38. To Everything, Turn, Turn, Turn 134

39. Tell it Like it is IV (draft post) 137

40. Be a Happy Man. I Try the Best I Can 138

41. Blindly I Imagined I Could Keep You Under Glass 143

42. Never Knowing What Could Have Been 148

43. Angels With Silver Wings, Shouldn't Know Suffering 151

44. These are Days You'll Remember 154

45. No One Believed the Water Would Come 157

46. Tell it Like it is V 160

47. Time, Time, Time 161

Year 5 {or the year I traded in my bucket of pain for a spoonful of wisdom}.....165

48. Things Change, Yet They Stay the Same 172

49. Hello, It's Me 174

50. Never Let Me Slip, 'Cause if I Slip, Then I'm Slippin' 177

51. And Maybe Someday We Will Find That it Really Wasn't Wasted Time 182

52. Out on a Limb 185

53. You and Tequila 189

54. Got to Keep My Irons in the Fire 194

55. Check Yo-Self Before You Wreck Yo-Self 197

56. Happy Birthday, E 202

57. Cold as Ice 203

Epilogue 205

Dedicated to Ethan.
You came into my life and delivered many gifts.
I will forever be grateful for each and every one of them.

INTRODUCTION

There are some things in life that are simply unimaginable. I would put *losing your 30 year old husband in an instant* on that list of very unimaginable things.

Losing a spouse at any age is a devastating and difficult ordeal that leads to an often devastating and difficult (and sometimes unbearably long) journey. How we get through that ordeal and the journey that follows is about as unique to each one of us as our fingerprints. Along with screaming in the car while sitting in traffic (it was LA, everyone else was doing it, so I hardly seemed out of place), throwing things (mostly at walls, but I may or may not have thrown a thing or two at a living being, my recollection is a bit fuzzy - that's my story, and I'm stickin to it), and binge shopping (a subject for another book entirely), the thing that I found most cathartic was to write.

Whether I was, or am, any good at it wasn't really the point at the time. I got feelings out "on paper", or in my case "online", that I could never talk to my family or friends about. Not because I don't have wonderful family and friends (they are the best, honest), it's just that I simply couldn't sit face to face and verbalize my feelings as well as I could when I was alone with my laptop and my own thoughts, which generally occurred at some ungodly hour (my grief journey was rife with insomnia).

I started out in the beginning blogging on MySpace. Yes, you read that right - this was back in 07 when blogging wasn't de rigueur (every celebrity, mommy, chick with a camera, and young widow didn't already have one). I laugh as I look back and see some of the posts referring to MySpace, which make me feel like an absolute dinosaur. But, I had a place to write, so write I

Life ain't always beautiful, but it's one hell of a ride...

did. A few of my friends did in fact log in and read what I wrote, and I felt good about being able to communicate to some of the people in my life about how I was feeling, albeit in a bit of a cowardly way. I eventually found a *real* blogging platform, and others outside of family and friends eventually discovered my blog. I think that was the point at which I began to pay closer attention to my actual writing skills. Writing in my blog and journaling my grief and journey toward healing helped me to grow in many ways - expected and not so expected.

I wrote when I was upset, confused, or uncertain. I wrote when my kids did stuff and I had no one else to tell, really, my husband no longer being here with me to celebrate. I wrote when I had breakdowns and I wrote when I had break*throughs*. My blog became my connection to the outside world, where I discovered there were other people who had lost spouses, too. It was both sad and comforting to discover that I wasn't alone in being young and widowed, left here on my own with children to raise, a mortgage to pay, and mouths to feed all by myself. But it was through my writing that I felt heard above the emotional, and sometimes physical, chaos that had suddenly become my life, and that made me feel a lot less alone on my journey.

This book is a collection of selected posts from my first blog "Changing Lanes". I decided to create this book from those years of posts to provide the same stories and information in a more organized and orderly fashion (again, a nod to the ever present chaos). In addition, the stories - or posts - contained in this book are in ascending order, so they start at the beginning of my story, as opposed to the reverse as they appear on the blog. While all posts have been reviewed and edited for grammar and all of that good stuff, they have not been edited for content, and appear here as close as possible to the way they were originally written.

Life ain't always beautiful, but it's one hell of a ride...

Another point worth noting, that you will soon discover, is that there is a deep connection to music throughout. I spent years of my life both before and after my husband's death working in the music and entertainment industry in Los Angeles. But long before that, I had a deep love of music that goes all the way back to early childhood, when I would marvel at the album covers of my father's record collection. There was always music in a wide variety of genres in our home, and I would sit for hours with my father listening to records. He had an incredible love of music, and his appreciation for a wide and incredibly varied range of styles was shared with me and came to greatly influence my life and career, something I am very thankful for. Not only did it provide me with a rich musical education that would eventually lead me down the path toward working in the music industry, but I have a prevalent and rich soundtrack to just about every stage of my life, with most memories being more noted for the songs I loved at the time, than whatever was actually happening in my life at that time. Now, I hear a song and am immediately transported to a time or an event in my past, as I find myself submerged in the rhythms, sounds, and lyrics of a song I may not have heard literally in decades.

As a teen, I spent several years moving back and forth between Los Angeles and the UK, and while that may seem pretty awesome now, the experience resulted in me being exceptionally lonely during those important formative years. While friends and one's social life were everything to most adolescent girls, I was the weird foreigner at school; because of that, I struggled a great deal to make friends, of which I had very few. But that was okay, I had my music to keep me company. It would be the first time that I realized that music could entertain and understand, and it could also provide glorious escape from the negative things in life. And music has been keeping me company ever since, seeing me through all of my journeys – the good, the bad, and the incredibly ugly.

The artists that I shared my time with understood me, knew what I was feeling, or told a story so vividly, I was transported to a much better place than my reality at the time. Music was my constant companion, my therapy. So it isn't any wonder that when I found myself thrust into one of the darkest times of my adult life, it was music that I turned to in search of solace and understanding. And this explains the story/post titles: even now I can reach for a song, or a simple line of lyric, to express my deepest thoughts and feelings. For me, music has never been something you just listen to, some sort of background noise at the gym or the grocery store. Music is art, and art is life.

The song titles (and few lyrics) included here all hold meaning to me. Sometimes the line or lyric would pop into my head as I was writing. Sometimes I had heard a line in a song that day, and found it so profound that I actually was prompted to expand upon an idea that sprung from that individual line. Sometimes I was so overwhelmed by my grief, I let someone else's lyrics do the talking, knowing that talented songwriters could put into words my feelings far better than I – as they had done for so many moments in my life before. I have a great amount of gratitude to those songwriters, both for their art, and for unknowingly helping this particular widow through what would prove to be the most difficult journey of her life.

YEAR 1

{ or: that year some really crazy shit went down }

As post-loss years go for the young and widowed, most will agree that the first year is pretty much the worst. This is, of course, arguable depending upon who you ask and where they happen to be on their journey (we will get to year two soon enough), but every day, every milestone, each important (and unimportant) event experienced without your love by your side is brand spanking new, and thus, so are your feelings and reactions, and the feelings and reactions of those who make up your support system of family members, friends, and peers. You don't know what to think or do – and neither do they. And rarely will anyone be in a position to help guide this grief ship. It is literally a case of "the blind leading the blind", and no one has any real idea where you are all headed.

You hear people talk about "the year of firsts". This would be the collective experience of the first time you celebrate your – or your deceased partner's – birthday, the first time you celebrate your wedding anniversary, first Christmas/new year/kids' birthday(s), etc., without your partner by your side. All of these dreaded firsts lead up to the granddaddy of all firsts: the first anniversary of your late spouse's death.

As luck would have it, I got my very first "first" out of the way immediately, as in *the very next day* following the incident in which my husband was killed. You see, he was killed the day before our wedding anniversary. Each and every year since his death I have had the occasion to celebrate one of the best days of my life and what was undoubtedly the worst day of my life – conveniently packaged back to back, and most often falling on the President's Day holiday weekend.

By the time I began writing in Changing Lanes, I was just shy of 6 months into what would become a very long and tedious personal journey. I had just gone back to work full-time after a nearly 5 month absence, time I was very grateful (and privileged) to have had. However, in a business where my husband and I worked together so often, in an industry where we knew all of the same people (who obviously were well aware of what had happened), I was ill prepared for the questions and the awkwardness of encountering so many of my peers for the first time since his funeral. It was so weird that they were just then - upon interacting with me for the first time after so many months - having to deal with something that I had been working on adjusting to for months at that point. Every phone call began (on the other end) with, "Oooh... how *are* you?" And I managed to do a pretty good job of not replying, "Oh, I don't know. Husband's dead, I'm swimming in a pile of debt, haven't slept in about 6 months, everyone has gone back to their lives and just *left* me here... But other than that I'm great!" I knew that nothing that happened was their fault. Nothing that had occurred could in any way be fixed by them, and nothing they said would make me feel any better, no matter how well thought out, or well intentioned it might have been on their part. At least when I went to work I had someone else to talk to, other than my toddler and the dog, and, of course, the voices inside my own head, which seemed to multiply every time I turned the lights out at night. And I can look back now and say at least they cared enough to actually ask how I was. But before I would get to this point, some really crazy shit went down. This is probably a really good time to fill you in...

* * * *

My journey began on Saturday, February 17, 2007. At the time my husband and I were living in Los Angeles, in the beautiful home we had just purchased five short months before, located in a quiet suburb west of the city.

Life ain't always beautiful, but it's one hell of a ride...

We both were enjoying success and steady upward growth in our respective careers, I at a small but successful music label and management company, and my husband as a recording and mix engineer.

We were both very fortunate in that we worked with some of the world's most recognized musical artists, and enjoyed the benefits of those associations and the steady work those clients brought. From every observable angle, we were well on our way to living the American dream. We couldn't in our wildest imagination conceive of the swift and violent manner in which that dream would ~~unravel~~ be shattered.

It was Saturday, and it also happened to be the first day of the long President's Day weekend, a rare 3 day block of time off for me, perfectly timed to coincide with our wedding anniversary, which happened to fall on the Monday holiday. As is not uncommon for Southern California even in the winter, it was a nice day out, and I had hoped to spend the day together as a family – Ethan, myself, and our 18 month old toddler (my eldest daughter was at the time away in Michigan with her biological father). Maybe we'd hang around the house for a while before finding something interesting enough to make us go through the tactical planning and packing ordeal necessary to get out of the house with a toddler. I was happy that for once we had a weekend where neither of us was committed to work, and I was looking forward to enjoying the moment. Ethan, it seemed, had other plans.

The preceding weekend we had attended the Grammy Awards, where Ethan had been a nominee for his contribution to an album that had been nominated for "Album of the Year". It was a very exciting time for us both, as you can imagine. And while the accolades were never the end game, he had made a quiet personal goal of being nominated for a Grammy by the time he was 30. The nominations were announced a week before his 30th birthday in

December, and his name was on the list. Calling my husband that morning to let him know about his nomination was, hands down, the best phone call I ever got to make in my entire career. In typical Ethan fashion, he was only made more humble by the honor, barely able to bring himself to announce the fact to friends he'd called to tell – quickly sliding it in at the end of the conversation ("so, yeah, I'll call you Friday about getting together to watch the game. Oh, and, uh, I got nominated. Alright, later man..."). Perhaps he just didn't quite believe it himself, but I just think he felt uncomfortable talking about his professional accomplishments. He'd much rather sit and listen to you talk about yours.

It was this very personality trait of his – this ability to always remain humble – that would piss me off that particular Saturday. As he bounded down the stairs dressed in an actual *shirt* shirt, and a hat on his head, I knew something was up (the man had more hair on his head than anyone you've ever met, yet he refused to leave the house without a darn baseball cap on. I never understood it, but it was his *thing*, what can you do...). And it turns out I was right. He was headed out to the Record Plant to do a mix for a potential new client. This would normally be a cause for celebration, weekend or not; after all, life as an independent engineer is not easy, and you take (and celebrate) the work as it comes, but this was a *spec* mix and it was ruining my weekend for a couple of reasons:

It was Saturday, it was our anniversary weekend, and *it was a spec mix.* When you work on spec, you do the work and if the client likes it, they accept it and pay you for it. If they don't like it, you've just spent a day (or two) of your life on something that you make no money on. And when I say "a day or two", I mean it – 12-14 hours per day for a couple of days is not unusual for a mix.

Someone who had just been nominated for a Grammy, in my opinion, shouldn't have to turn around the following weekend and do a mix on spec. I felt my husband's humble nature was being taken advantage of.

So, I was annoyed that he wanted to work when I wanted to enjoy some nice family time, but I was *pissed off* because he wasn't even going to get paid for the exchange. I tried reasoning with him about the issue, but it did no good. The studio was booked and he'd already told the (perspective) client he was going in. Then fate attempted to intervene…

E: Hey, Stephie, have you seen the disc with the session files for _____?

Me: (disinterested) Nope. Where'd you leave it?

E: I thought I left it on the counter, but it's not here…

Me: (without looking up) Yeah, I haven't seen it…

Ethan began searching the house calmly… after about 10 minutes of looking in the usual spots (the car, his editing space upstairs, the catch-all kitchen counter, his backpack), he started to become a little more frantic. Feeling bad for him, I got up and began to look around, too. My husband's work was very important to him, and it was to me, too. He was worried that he'd have to call the (potential) client and cancel, being forced to admit that he had misplaced the disc with the files. That apparent act of irresponsibility was not a good place to start a relationship with a client, and, since I was often in the position of "client" in these types of situations, I knew this all too well. Suddenly I started to sympathize with him.

As Ethan went out to check the car… *again*… I started going through the family room in closer detail. As he and I went about the house picking up things, moving things around, in search of this disc, our 18 month old sat quietly in her little mini wingchair watching Sprout. Looking back on it, I swear

Life ain't always beautiful, but it's one hell of a ride…

she would have probably started whistling in melodramatic fashion had she learned the skill yet, but, alas, she hadn't, and instead sat there nonchalantly, ignoring the tiny hint of panic that was beginning to seep into the room. Looking at her, I had the sudden notion to look through the cabinet and see if the disc had been accidentally stored away with her many dvds (and our piles of cds and god knows whatever else) in the tv cabinet. After taking everything out (who knew there was so much crap in there?) and sifting through the discs one by one, I ultimately came up empty. However, as I was putting (okay, shoving) the "stuff" back into the cabinet, my eyes at the same level as the bottom of the dvd player, something caught my eye. I saw something glistening at the very back of the tv cabinet.

Pulling out the dvd player from its cozy little space, I found shoved in the very back of the narrow space, the missing dvd. Locating that thing was a serious miracle because we all know that I did not regularly clean that space (okay, I never cleaned that space, but, still…), it could have been back there for months before anyone rescued it. I looked at the disc, and looked at my toddler – she is the only one who could possibly have put it under there, but the question to this day remains, *how*? It's important to note here, that this was a corner television cabinet for an "old school" 40-something-inch television, not a flat screen. The distance between the front of the cabinet to the back of the cabinet was quite great. She was too little to pull the dvd player out and put it back there, and perfectly replace the dvd player. The only way for her to have gotten it back there would have been to line it up on the shelf, and give it a perfect, strong, push to send it all the way to the back. But she had no history of doing that, nothing else was found back there with the disc, and nothing else was ever discovered back there as long as we continued to have that cabinet in the room. This mystery, and whether or not

Life ain't always beautiful, but it's one hell of a ride…

my toddler was associated with it, would haunt me for a long time (still kind of does), but in that moment, I was happy to be able to save the day for my husband, who was equally puzzled by the disc's location.

With the reality that, in fact, he was heading out the door to work (on spec, in case anyone forgot), sinking in, in a little mini-huff I resumed my place on the sofa. Ethan thanked me for my help, quickly grabbed his backpack, and headed out the front door. I could hear the car start in the driveway. And then moments later he burst through the front door.

"Did you forget something?" I asked. He was walking down the entry hall straight toward me.

"Yes," he replied, "I forgot to tell my wife I love her."

He leaned over and kissed me on the mouth. As we parted, he gave me one of those big giant grins of his that made his whole lovely face light up. I had no idea that would be the last time I would ever kiss my husband.

As is typical he spent a very long day (and night) in the studio, working well into the wee hours of the next morning. As was also typical, at least on the weekends, I stayed up to wait for his return. This would usually occur anytime between 2-4am. Looking at the clock, I noticed that it was 4:16am. Unable to keep my eyes open any longer, and knowing Ethan would likely arrive any moment, I decided to head up to bed.

Well, I was right. At that very moment, he was indeed on his way home. Unfortunately unbeknownst to him, a young man who had been out celebrating his birthday that evening with friends was driving intoxicated (nearly twice the legal limit) on that same stretch of highway. After driving for a while west-bound on the 101 Hollywood freeway, the young man, who I would later know by the name Greggory McMillion, inexplicably pulled over to the right shoulder, paused momentarily, and in a decision that would change many lives forever, proceeded to make a u-turn and head the wrong way - traveling full speed - into opposing traffic. According to witness accounts, he passed several cars as he traveled at them at speeds estimated to be near or above 80 mph. At 4:16am on Sunday, February 18, 2007, the same time I saw the clock and felt my husband was on his way home to me and our daughter, Greggory McMillion rounded a bend traveling eastbound in the fast lane of the westbound side of the freeway, and struck my husband's vehicle head on.

Mr. McMillion survived the collision, relatively unscathed. My husband, however, was killed instantly upon impact.

What happened next was, really, nothing more than a wild, crazy, unbelievable *blur*. There were phone calls, and lots of people... and police. There were Coroners and District Attorneys, and courtrooms.

There would be months and months of hearings of all sorts, witnesses, lawyers and toxicologists.

There were many, many unanswered, and unanswerable, questions.

And countless tears.

There was the blatant, in-your-face realization that this shit actually happens in real life... *to me*... to *US*... not just to other people I saw on TV.

And this is where this collection of posts, and this long journey begin...

1

GOTTA START SOMEWHERE...
{ August 7, 2007 }

Just under 6 months ago my beautiful husband was killed in an automobile crash (I won't call it an accident). In the early morning hours of February 18, 2007, a wrong way drunk driver who was traveling against traffic in the fast lane of the US101 freeway here in Los Angeles struck and killed him. Apparently he died instantly, though I have a hard time finding peace with that, and always wonder if he suffered before he passed away.

I will never forget the phone call I received from the coroner's office (yes, phone call) at 8AM on that Sunday morning. When the phone rang, it woke me up. I instantly noticed that I was in bed alone, however, it wasn't unusual, due to my husbands work hours, he was either still at the studio, or had maybe fallen asleep on the couch downstairs like he'd done on previous occasions (he'd come home still "wired" from work and sit and surf the web. I'd come down in the morning to find him curled up with his laptop on the couch...). Then I was struck with an angry thought as I reached for the phone, thinking "I can't believe these telemarketers are calling at 8AM on a SUNDAY morning!"... There was a woman on the other end of the phone who asked me if I was Stephanie Cooper. Once I confirmed that, she asked me if I was related to Ethan Willloughby. "yes" I said, "who is this". "Are you his wife?" she continued. "Yes, who ARE you and why are you calling?" I was getting angry

Life ain't always beautiful, but it's one hell of a ride...

at this "telemarketer" for the line of questioning and was about to tell her to "f"-off when she replied that she was "xxx" from the Los Angeles Coroner's Office and that my husband had been in an accident.

The words "coroner's office" echoed in my brain.

Immediately I cut her off: "where is my husband?" I couldn't breathe.

"Your husband was in an accident."

"WHERE is my husband?"

"I'm sorry... He passed away".

"Who IS this" I said again. I was sure that this was the cruelest, most disgusting prank anyone had ever pulled.

"This is xxx from the LA Coroner's Office" she said again.

I only remember pieces of the conversation with the woman on the phone after this point. I recall her saying my name repeatedly as I lay on the floor unable to breathe. I began, literally, to convulse. The baby began to cry. I was all alone with a 1 year old and I couldn't move. I was paralyzed. I was ill.

I remember her wanting to call my in-laws in Wisconsin, and having a moment of clarity, I yelled, "Don't you do that to them! You find someone to go to their house!"

And I remember being totally and completely alone for the first time (of what would be many) for those 5 minutes it took for her to call the sheriff's department in my husband's little home town to request that they dispatch someone to my in-laws' home to deliver the news that their son had been killed.

I remember her asking me if there was someone I could call to be with me, and I remember calling my mother with my cell phone (always by the bed...) while she stayed on the other phone. I remember my mom answering and I never forget our conversation:

Life ain't always beautiful, but it's one hell of a ride...

Mom: "hello"

Me: "Mommy Ethan"

Mom: "What's the matter"

Me: "Mommy Ethan was in an accident"

Mom: "Okay. He's going to be okay" (she was trying to console me. I DO tend to overreact sometimes...)

Me: "No Mommy"

Mom: "Okay, Stephie, it's going to be okay"

Me: "NO Mommy! Ethan's DEAD!"

I remember her screaming "Oh my God! I'm coming, I'll be right there!"

"Right there" was a 30 minute drive. 30 minutes that felt like an eternity.

So I waited with the stranger on the phone. That horrible, evil person that had brought this news that ruined our lives.

I remember my mother walking through the door and I collapsed onto the floor, dropping the phone, which my step-father was there to catch. He could talk to the devil, I absolutely could not spend another minute on the phone with her.

Somewhere in there I had gotten my crying 1 year old out of her crib and I think I changed her diaper... The next thing I remember was sitting on the couch and my mom slapping at my face. I guess I'd passed out, or at least gone completely catatonic... Funny thing is, having another brief moment of clarity after all the face slapping, I asked my mother to call a family member who owns a cleaning company.

There'd be people coming, the house was a mess...

Then the people... in twos and fours... with food... The phone calls (an autopsy...? For a homicide caused by a drunk driver...? To rule out MY

Life ain't always beautiful, but it's one hell of a ride...

HUSBAND being the cause...? I'm sorry, but he was on the RIGHT side of the freeway... Oh yeah, the jury...)

The tears I cried that day, you'd think that you would run out of them after hours and hours and HOURS of crying, but the body is an amazing machine, and miraculously can create as many tears as you can manage to cry.

The time after that was a blur. I know my in-laws showed up from Wisconsin the next day. Then his best friend from Chicago. Then his God brother and his wife. There was a walk through of the site in Malibu we'd be having a memorial service...

Memorial Service... It's still not right...

We'd follow that memorial service with a trip to Wisconsin for the funeral. It never seemed to end, but we had to do something for his friends and ~~my~~ our family in Los Angeles, even though I knew I couldn't bury my husband anywhere but in Wisconsin. He came to LA to follow a dream of working in Music, at which he succeeded, gaining his first Grammy nomination shortly before his death. We'd just been at his first, last, and only Grammy Awards exactly one week before he passed away. But even with all of his accomplishments, he was just a small town kid from Wisconsin, and he LOVED it there. If it had anything to do with beer, brats, Packers, Badgers or Brewers, he was all about it. And I will always respect that. I do regret that I can't go and visit him, and I often feel guilty that he's so far away. I hope that he's okay with my decision.

I spend a lot of time these days talking to him. I tell him how much I miss him. How much I love him. Alone at night in my room, I often find myself begging him for hours to come home. At least I've stopped waiting for him to walk through the front door, even though I wish he would. I look at his photos everyday and I am scared about what lies ahead for me and my girls. I probably need therapy, but what I would prefer is someone to talk to that's already been where I am and where I'm going (I don't want someone to sit with their notepad and ask me "how are you doing today?"), so I try to seek those people out. Maybe it's stupid, I don't know, but I do know that I need to do something. Things don't get any easier, at least they haven't for me. The justice system is another blog entry for another day, but the trial is looming and I'm very, very scared that this murderer is going to get nothing more than the proverbial slap on the wrist. But again, more on that another time...

I titled this post "Gotta Start Somewhere" because I've been thinking of starting a blog for, oh, about 5 months now. Suddenly I guess the stars aligned tonight, so... well... here I am. I'll be around regularly, usually to rant, because there is really nothing more you can do in these situations (did you expect comedy?). If you want me to grin and bear it, show up to my office during business hours, Monday through Friday. This is not the time or place for it, this is my place to be honest, and I intend to be nothing less here...

Life ain't always beautiful, but it's one hell of a ride...

2

I MISS YOU
{ August 9, 2007 }

Ethan:

Today I was walking in the mall with the girls, wasting time waiting for our food from California Pizza Kitchen (silly me, I shoulda called first, I know...). Anyway, Ava was running around with a big pie eatin' grin on her face and Mychaela and I were trying to pass an old couple but we couldn't because there was too much stuff down the middle of the walkway... I realized after a few moments that the woman had just been carrying on non-stop the entire time. The couple were probably in their 70's, at least, and they were holding hands walking through the mall and the woman was blabbing his ear off (in Spanish). Occasionally he'd chime in "mm-hhmm" or something like that. All I could think of was you. And then us. And that we would never be 70 and holding hands walking through the mall, me talking your ear off about something (probably my bunions) and you just saying "mm-hhmm". Until, of course, you got tired of the mall and started your "where's the layaway department" routine in the middle of Nordstrom. (BTW, I know I acted mortified when you did that, but I only reacted that way because you were so very pleased with yourself for embarrassing me. I really thought it was funny).

I miss you desperately. When I saw that couple today, I almost cried. I don't understand why God lets some people have each other for so long, yet others get one another for a mere moment. It's not fair. It's really not fair...

I love you a million times,
Stephie

3

MINDFUL OF ONE'S MATTERS
{ August 13, 2007 }

The psyche is such a strange thing. We have no control over it, it seams, regardless of whether or not we "think we know better", or try to follow the mantra "mind over matter". Truth is, matter will always matter where the mind is concerned and there's not a darn thing you can do about it.

It's so strange how one day can be really hard to get through and the very next day can be okay. That's not to say that there is ever a day that goes by that I don't think of Ethan, but I am able to do it without falling apart sometimes, and other times the smallest thing can trigger a memory that sends me into a tail spin. For example, some days Ava can accomplish a new milestone and I can smile and hug her and think about how proud her dad would be, other days a similar accomplishment will cause me to cry and hold her as I think of how proud her dad would be...

I get told, or it is insinuated to me, often that I need to "relax", that I "can't do anything about it, so deal with it". I'm supposed to shut off my mind's natural propensity - to grieve, to worry about my children, my finances, the future of my family and home situation - and override it's pre-wired behavior by telling myself that I'm okay? I'm supposed to lie to myself until I've talked myself into believing those lies to be true. I don't know if I can do that. To talk myself into believing I'm okay would be to talk myself into believing that what happened to Ethan was okay, and it's not and never will be. That fact brings me to the conclusion that I will never be okay. I am doomed to be trapped in this prison of emotion for the rest of my life, and I don't know what to do about it... Like a really God-awful roller coaster that I can't ever get off.

I just want to get off...

Life ain't always beautiful, but it's one hell of a ride...

4

DREAM A LITTLE DREAM
{ August 16, 2007 }

In the last few days I've spent a lot of time on the internet, mostly seeking out others like myself that are in dire need of other people to speak to about their feelings and their loss. I've stumbled upon the saddest, most heartbreaking "club" you could ever know, one who's membership consists of reluctant, unwitting women and men, some unbelievably, and sadly, very young, the common denominator being the collective "unimaginable".

There are those for whom much time has past but the pain still runs deep and the emotion is still like a fast moving river that time can't seem to slow down. Then there are those who are taking steps large (re-marriage) and small ("I left the house today") to try to reconstruct what remains of their dismantled lives, shaken to the core by events they couldn't control, like a small town after a catastrophic earthquake. There are those that are new to this club and need guidance and support from those who have come before them, and many of those "club elders" are more than happy to reach out their hands for those of us to grasp a hold of. This simple act of human kindness has struck me as quite remarkable. I have seen many, many postings of widows saying "please reach out to me if you'd like to chat" "or email me if you need anything", and, unlike the common-folk, these people actually mean it. You see: they know what it's like to have people tell you those things and NOT mean them, so they wouldn't imagine uttering those words themselves unless they truly did.

I've often sat and wondered what these people were like before this "experience". I wonder how it changed them as a person. Not their lives - we all can just imagine how drastically most aspects of their lives have changed – but their *actual person*. What kind of person were they before, compared to now. Some of these people are so compassionate and willing to help, were they so before?

Experiencing a loss such as this, the loss of a spouse, can put so many things into perspective in a way that many of us couldn't imagine beforehand. You find that which matters most begins to crystallize before you. The concept of time becomes very apparent, which I think is a major thing that changes for most of the younger people that find themselves walking this particular road. Until reality is thrust upon us, we tend to believe that not only are we going to live forever, but also that we are going to live out all of our days with our partner, who's going to live forever, too. We make plans for the vacation we're going to take, not next year, but the year after that. What we're going to do when we retire, and so on… Now that's not to say that you shouldn't make plans, however, I guess I am just a little more reluctant to believe in the future, so I may as well not waste time planning for one.

I spend most of my time these days thinking about what will happen to my children if I die. When I think of the future that is what I think about. Morbid, I know, but it's my reality. I have no faith that tomorrow is going to arrive (and I usually curse it when it does), so I try not to think about it because when I do, it's never positive. I guess that's the biggest thing that's changed about me. I am an Aquarius, we're well known dreamers. Dreaming is part of my makeup, part of who I am. But my ability to dream has dissipated, and I don't know if I will ever witness its return. Ethan would probably be very upset to hear me say that. We were dreamers together, he and I. That's what we did, that was our bond (well, that and a secret passion for 80's hair metal, shhh, don't tell anyone…). We dreamed about our family - our kids going to college. We dreamed about our home - about that deck we were going to build, and the hot tub we were going to install (when we got rid of that God forsaken radio tower – looong story for another day). We dreamed of the long and successful careers we were going to have, of our future achievements.

We were a team, and we were truly each other's biggest fans. I've never in all my years known what it was like to actually make someone proud of me until I met Ethan. He encouraged me at every turn, and stood beside me when I needed to follow my heart (whether it was the best financial decision or not). We looked forward to sitting in our house, complaining about "kids today" because we were 70, and, well, it would be our right…

But now it's all gone. And the dreaming has stopped. So that's what has changed about me the most, I guess. I've absolutely lost my ability to dream…

5

TOMORROW, YOU'RE ONLY A DAY AWAY
{ August 17, 2007 }

In less than a few hours, the clock will roll over to midnight. It will be August 18, marking 6 months since Ethan's passing. This has been looming over me for a couple of days, like a fierce storm on the horizon; you can see, it, you know it's coming, but maybe if you hope hard enough, it will make a quick right and leave you be. While this would not be impossible for even the most wicked of hurricanes, not so with the ticking of the clock. That next second is already destined to arrive and turn into a minute, an hour, a day... 6 months... And so it is there, staring me down, trying to "see what I'm made of".

But, Tomorrow, I'll save you the trouble. You win. Will you just leave me alone now if I throw up my hands? No need to pass through here, displaying your finery, "proving your points" and such. We both already know that you are greater than me. One portion of you, one moment, one tenth of one of your seconds, is greater than the whole of my parts. I can not handle you, Tomorrow.

To all of my friends, those of you who think that I am strong, that I'm a "tough cookie", that I'll be alright: I'm none of those things. Yesterday was a nightmare, I barely made it through today, and I think Tomorrow just may destroy me all over again...

Life ain't always beautiful, but it's one hell of a ride...

6

MEMORIES FADE, BUT THE SCARS STILL LINGER
{ August 24, 2007 }

It's been a while since I last posted something, so I thought it was high time to revisit my blog. I've been really down in the dumps lately and not felt much like writing because... well... not that any of the previous stuff is HAPPY, but I think this has been one of my lowest points in a while and literally nothing that comes out of my mouth (or the tips of my fingers, as it were) is positive in any way, shape, or form.

I'm starting to feel things that I didn't feel before. I mean, I've been reeling in grief since 8AM February 18th, however, I'm suddenly very aware of it all, in such an astonishingly BIG way. It's like standing in front of me staring at me, when I step right, it steps left, when I step left, it steps right. Laughing. Just laughing at me. "Hahahaha! You can't get past me"...

I've read from some other widows that I've become acquainted with over this miraculous thing we call the internet, that, contrary to the idea that time inherently causes you to feel better, sometimes when you get to that 6 month or 1 year mark things can sometimes seem worse than they were previously. I guess that's about the time the numbness starts to wear off and reality starts to actually sink in. I think perhaps, that's where I am at. I think the reality of Ethan being gone is actually beginning to become apparent in so many ways. That's not to say that I wasn't missing him before, that's not what I

Life ain't always beautiful, but it's one hell of a ride...

mean. This is about having to make an effort to remember what he felt like, or smelled like, or what his voice sounded like because our memories, as sophisticated as they are, are not as powerful as our bodies' natural healing mechanism. Look at it like this: you fall down and you get a cut. What happens? You bleed. It scabs over - you can see it so you know the wound is there, though the actual injury is behind you. The scab disappears in time, replaced by skin - you remember the wound but it doesn't actually "hurt" anymore. That spot will never be the same again since the skin has been mingled with scar tissue. Eventually that scar will fade with time. Not completely going away, but sometimes you actually have to look for it, or only notice it when someone (or something) points it out as a reminder. I would suppose that the healing of the surface of the skin is not that different than the healing of the heart...

Thing is, as much as I want to remember everything about him, I also want to heal. I don't know how you can do both because one, just by nature, works against the other. Again, I don't mean to say that you ever forget entirely. But you start to forget some of the things that sometimes you are so desperate not to. I don't want to have to remember those sensations, I want them to still be real, like they have been. But, now those sensations are beginning to become distant, and I am starting to fear that in time they will disappear altogether. What is this new level of emptiness that I have to look forward to? This absolute vacancy... With guilt to boot (shouldn't I always feel his touch or hear his voice, on command, by my own minds desire?)...

Here's a little tid-bit that I've told a few people in the last day or so, but I'll put it here for the rest of you... I recently had some work done on the house. Stuff that REALLY needed to get done, and it looks WONDERFUL, Ethan would have been very pleased indeed. Anyway, not the point... So

Life ain't always beautiful, but it's one hell of a ride...

while they were there finishing up some drywall work in our master bathroom, I guess they noticed a little DIY patchwork on the wall in the master bedroom (you really couldn't help notice it, it's right next to the door at "eye level" and was not painted, so was a big white square…). Well, I guess they thought since they had the plaster out, they would fix it up for me (without asking). When I got home, I went upstairs to look at the work in the bathroom. When coming out of my room, I noticed that they had corrected the hole-patching job next to the door. It took my breath away and I had to keep myself from crying. The next day when they came back to finish their work, I said to the contractor, "I see you fixed the patch job by the door." "Yes," he said, "we had the plaster and the drywall, so we went ahead and fixed it for you". Now, under normal circumstances I would have thanked him profusely. However, not today.

You see, Ethan put a lovely, ahem, fist sized hole in that wall back in about January. Yeah, I can be a little hard to live with sometimes (a few of you may be familiar with the sharpness of my tongue), and… well… I guess I really pissed him off that day… anyway, about a week later he "fixed" the hole in the wall with a little drywall and a whole bunch more plaster than necessary. "Look what I did" I remember him saying with a huge smile on his face. I looked. The wall looked pregnant. It was hilarious! But that was him: great mixer, *really bad handy* man. So, as much as I knew that one day I would like to have had the wall fixed properly, I wasn't ready for it yet. Every day I would look at that bad patch job and laugh and remember how much he wanted to be a husband, a father, caretaker of our homestead, and though he wasn't exactly the next Bob Villa, he would always be ready and willing to get out a hammer (fun!) or the drill and put something up (usually crooked) or whatever, always a willing victim to my home decorating madness (well, I don't know how "willing" he

was, but he would just smile and go "get it out of the car because I can't lift it".
To make matters worse, he was usually tricked into assembling whatever it was, too (always a sucker for the batting eyelashes).

So I guess my point is, when I walk out of my bedroom now, I look at where there used to be a memory of my husband, and all I see now is perfectly smooth drywall. Yet another piece of him stripped away, I was totally not prepared for it, nor having to "search" for the memory of his embrace…

7

CONFIDENCE IN HIGH SPEED
{ August 26, 2007 }

For six months I've been trying to figure out "why" this had to happen to Ethan. To me. To Ava. To Ethan's parents, two of the most selfless, lovely people you could ever meet, and to Mychaela. And I run through the range of emotions: anger, sadness, fear, guilt, powerlessness, anxiety, depression... You name it. If it's "negative" I feel it on a daily basis. Probably a couple-a-times-a-daily-basis. However, every once in a while there will be a moment of clarity. Always a very brief moment, as the positive thoughts always give way to a river of tears, but for a moment of my life I can think positive thoughts while looking back on the relationship between Ethan and I before we got to this... wretched... place...

Our relationship got off to a bit of a slow roll. Actually, and so many of you already know this, our relationship started off going backwards. We actually had a fight the first time we met. Ethan and I would later talk about this night and laugh hysterically. It was such nonsense. I won't share here, but, trust, it's pretty funny. Anyway, a few months would pass before we would find ourselves in each others company once more, and I'm so very glad we did, though it would still be a while before I would realize that. I know there was a bit of effort on the part of a couple of our friends, but I was a very reluctant participant in this dance. I was older. I had a kid. I wanted a serious

Life ain't always beautiful, but it's one hell of a ride...

relationship. He worked in Music. Nope, it would never work. But suddenly he was around a lot, and I got to know him a little better. So funny. And sweet. With beautiful eyes and an enormous smile. So finally on one fateful All Hallows Eve, I decided, before venturing out, that I was being silly and this was a man who really wanted to get to know on a more personal basis. Since that night, I can count on my hands the number of days that we spent apart. WE were instant. There was not a day that went by that we didn't see one another, unless it was absolutely unavoidable.

That first Thanksgiving, barely a month later, was so lonely as he had a standing date with the fellas in Vegas. That would be their last Thanksgiving "hurrah". On that subject, I will apologize guys, I never meant to be the Yoko Ono to your annual blitz fest. Please know that it wasn't intentional... He went home for Christmas that year as well and we talked so much on the phone you would have thought he was on some worldwide expedition for years somewhere, not at his parent's house for 4 days. We would move in together very quickly by most standards. That same year I became pregnant with Ava. We got married, and several months later welcomed our little muffin. The year following that, we bought our first (and last) house and settled in for a nice quiet ride into the sunset of our lives.

We packed a lot into 4 years. It was like the relationship X-Games, from beginning to end it was fast and very extreme. We loved each other deeply, completely and intensely. Sometimes we fought intensely as well. It wasn't always rosy at our house. For all the kindness in his eyes, he was exceptionally impatient. And, if you're here, you probably know me, and, well, I probably don't have to explain to you just how bad my attitude can get. Those two things didn't jibe well sometimes, so every once in a while we'd mix it up a

Life ain't always beautiful, but it's one hell of a ride...

bit. But, regardless of all that, we never stopped loving each other. Not for a minute. There was no question…

I often think that, despite our slow beginnings, the fates knew that we were not destined to have one another for long. As if we were being pushed along by some unknown, unseen force for our love to be fast and be strong. We had to get it all in before we ran out of time. We had a 10 year relationship in about 4 years. I know and fully appreciate how very blessed I am to have had him in my life, to bear his child - our incredibly amazing little girl - and to have been given the opportunity to love him and be loved by him.

I love and miss him every second of every day...

8

ANGER IS AN ENERGY
{ September 19, 2007 }

Well... Once again, I've let a bit of time pass between blog posts. I've thought daily about what I should write, or what I wanted to convey, however, I just couldn't seem to find the words that really did justice to everything that I'm currently going through or feeling...

Some keywords that come to mind: fear, anxiety, sorrow, despair, nervousness, disgust... Anger...

Mr. Rotten was right. It absolutely IS an energy. Aside from my kids, it's pretty much what propels me through my day. And I won't apologize for it, at least not this week. If you've crossed my path in the last couple of weeks, look for the fruit basket after NEXT week, okay, 'cause right now I just don't have it in me to say "sorry" to anyone...

The thing that is looming overhead now is the sentencing of the bastard that made this whole mess - the stupid, STUPID, selfish, sorry excuse for a human being that snatched Ethan away and threw my entire world off its axis. On Friday, September 21, Greggory McMillion Jr. (of [.....], if anyone is interested) will be sentenced to some measly little pittance of a sentence for what amounts to murder. I am so absolutely anxious. I feel sick and can't breathe. We'll see what I've got on Friday, I suppose, but this week has been really rough. It's like I get over one hurdle and here comes another... I got past

Life ain't always beautiful, but it's one hell of a ride...

the 6-month mark – horrible. Still reeling... Then came a "false start" on the guilty plea – it was entered 3 weeks ago, but there was a question about the charges/case law, and it was rescinded and the hearing held over for another week. Then two weeks ago came the guilty plea – "for real" this time. Then sentencing was scheduled, and now it is racing toward me at breakneck speed and I have no choice but to stand firm and face it. I feel like I'm constantly victimized by having to take part in this hideous nightmare from which I can not seem to wake to make an escape...

He pled guilty to two charges, and is currently facing a sentence of either 4/6/10 years. Since he has "no priors" we are facing an uphill battle in the "prison term" department. Since there was no trial (he pled out), the entire "human emotion" component is absent from the pool of information/knowledge/testimony that the judge will be taking into consideration when it comes time to make a decision about the sentence. I've already sat in court and heard her say (with my own ears!) that since he has "no priors", he "most likely won't be facing the maximum sentence". Now, how the hell are you going to sit in court, as the judge who is alone (no jury) in weighing the evidence and deciding the sentence of a murderer, and say something like that WITHOUT EVEN SERIOUSLY REVIEWING THE ENTIRE CASE??? It felt as if she had already made a decision based purely on his past, and not on WHAT HE DID, which was kill a human being!!! I will see how this all plays out, however, and if this kid gets a "slap on the wrist", this judge will definitely be looking at a formal complaint based on the transcripts of that hearing which, obviously, document her comment and show "bias" prior to review of the facts of the case. This is a person (though barely) who pulled over on the freeway. Sat on the shoulder. Contemplated what to do. Then proceeded to make a U-turn on a major U.S. highway. He avoided going the wrong way on the interchange, which is what he would have done if he REALLY wasn't aware of what he was doing (by the way, that's the defense: he was drunk, so he can't be held accountable for his actions because he couldn't have known what he was doing...), and then carried on down the highway at 75 miles-per-hour in the wrong direction in the fast lane.

There are many witness accounts from the preliminary hearing, and these, along with the police accounts and 911 calls are now the only "testimony" that can be considered. I, along with some of Ethan's family and friends, will make our best attempt to let the court know what kind of man Ethan was and how much we, and the world, lost when Ethan was killed. Though no one has been there the entire time to support him, most notably absent throughout the proceedings have been the wonderful friends of his that got him drunk and allowed him to drive all the way from North Hollywood to [.....] at almost twice the legal limit in the first place. They've all been sure to lay low, but now I'm sure that some of Mr. McMillion's family and friends will be there with bells on, to take the opportunity to stand up in court and tell the judge the usual: how he is such a "nice" boy, how this is an isolated incident, how he "didn't MEAN to kill anybody", how the knowledge of what he did is punishment enough and he should be sentenced lightly, etc. – all in an effort to downplay the fact that my husband was already sentenced to a life term, and by comparison, any sentence given to this guy under the current law is "getting off easy". A human life worth less than 10 years? I can not understand it. A judge that can proclaim that she concurs that a human life is worth less than 10 years? Even worse...

On that note, I have been pondering for a very long time what I will say that morning. I've had months to think about it, however, now that the actual time is upon me, I've suddenly become, well, overwhelmed with so many

Life ain't always beautiful, but it's one hell of a ride...

words and emotions that I can't straighten any of it out or make any sense of anything. Aside from telling Ethan that I loved him on Saturday, February 17th, these are probably going to be the most important words that will ever pass my lips. But what will I say? How do you sum up a man, a family, a lifetime of dreams and memories lost before we are given the opportunity to make them, all in a matter of minutes... all out in the open, for the world to hear... all to be heard and pondered as a matter of life or death? Okay, so the guy isn't facing a death sentence (no - that was given to Ethan), but this as close to redemption for Ethan's death as we are ever going to get. I guess I'd probably better stop writing here, and start organizing my thoughts as Friday will be here before you know it.

If you pray, please pray for my family. If you don't, but have considered it, now would be a GREAT time to take up the activity. If you regularly get spiritual advice from a rock in the backyard, your dog, or a tree, please share "positive thoughts" for us. Beggars can't be choosers and I'll take all the love I can get right now...

9

MY BABY SHE WROTE ME A LETTER
{ November 8, 2007 }

Dear Ethan:

I was just sitting here wallowing in my own sorrow, and I thought that I would just jot down a little note to you. So much has happened in the past couple of months, I'm sure you've been front row for it all, but if, by chance, you have happened to miss any of it, here we go…

The guy that ripped you away from us got 6 stinkin' years. I am told, with "good behavior" and "work credits" he can be out in 3.5 – 4 years. Goody for him, huh? There's so much to say about that day, but I just can't bring myself to re-live it all. The bottom line is, at least the guys in jail for a little while. I'm sure he'll make someone a lovely little bitch. Excuse me. Yes, I am somewhat angry. Just for you, I'll try to control myself…

I've been having a bit of trouble with the issue of restitution, and I have found myself submerged in case law and legal research. Something that I never thought I'd have to involve myself in. Your mind would be boggled by some of the most disgusting nonsense. People really want to get out of everything. No on wants to face the consequences of their actions, and the more that I research these cases, appeals, and whatnots, the sadder I become. I think what I'm most sad about is, that my case is not the most unjust there is. There are people here in California, and especially in other

Life ain't always beautiful, but it's one hell of a ride…

states where the laws are even more lax, that are literally getting away with murder. Literally. I am astounded.

Anyway, what that means to me is the criminal court doesn't want to require *the guy* to help me financially. They want to force my case into civil court. Unfortunately for them, I'm no idiot, and if I was angry before, now I'm absolutely PISSED and where I was asking for very little, I will now ask for everything I could possibly get my hands on by law, and I am finding that "by law" I could potentially get all of the restitution that I would seek in civil court as part of his criminal sentence. I have found some case law that supports this, and I have also found federal law that supports this as well. We'll see what the DA has to say, but since she is now, effectively, representing me and our family, she has to operate in my best interest one would figure (and one would highly recommend in this particular instance), so I have gotten a little more aggressive in terms of making sure that their office understands what my position is and that I know what my rights are under the California Constitution, and I will not allow them to dismiss me (or my rights).

I would hope that you are somewhere approving. It has taken pretty much all of my concentration, and I hope that those with whom I orbit in this great universe understand. This is a very important hurdle, and it could be the final hurdle in terms of my dealings with the criminal proceedings and could work out in a way that would allow me to put this part of our lives behind us and get on with the important work of healing in some way. Which leads me to this past Saturday…

I hung out with "the fellas" on Saturday. I guess I am glad that I did. I was very happy to be invited, I get so very lonely, and though I absolutely adore the girls, sometimes I just want to do "grown up things". At the last minute my fear of driving late at night was almost paralyzing. I was very close to calling and canceling, but I was afraid that if I didn't go, I wouldn't get invited again anytime soon, so off I went.

I really enjoyed their company, and laughed, which I don't do very much, so it was good. Of course, I couldn't even contemplate the idea of having as much as half a drink and driving home, so I had a nice… coffee… but that's alright, the company was more important. We played Uno and a little bit of poker. I think we were all equally as bad at both games, so it made it a pretty even playing field, which was good, kept everyone's attitudes in a good place. Played a couple of hands of poker before going home.

I was soooo scared driving home. I can't stand being out past 10 or so because I have this horrible fear that everyone on the road is drunk. As much as I've said to myself that I would rather be there with you than left here on my own, the fact is, I'm not on my own, I have the girls to think about and to take care of and I have the absolute worst fear of being in an accident and Ava having no one, and the girls being separated. I think it's bordering on paranoia, and at some point, when I can figure out where to find the time, I probably should see "someone" about it. Right now, I work and I come home and the thought of taking any more time away from the girls to do anything just doesn't seem fair to them. Anyway, I made it home okay, but I shook the whole way, nervous at every intersection that someone was going to come flying through it without stopping.

Anyway, when I got home I made myself a nice gin and tonic and went up to our room and… cried… and cried… and cried… While being with our friends was great, and I hope to do it more, it was the first time since you've been gone that I'd really gotten together with them like that and you weren't there, and it was just so wrong. So many things that I've had to adjust to doing without you, but I guess I just wasn't prepared for that or I didn't think about it because it's been so many months, I really got blindsided I guess. I miss you so terribly…

The rest you know. You have to know. I have to believe that you are with us, that you are with Ava and that you are aware of all of her amazing awesomeness. She's talking up a storm and saying the most "profound" things (okay, so maybe we'd be the only ones who think her saying "yes, Mommy, I'd like some oatmeal", or the fact that she is 2 and can spell and read her name – yeah, I know it's only 3 letters, but she's only 2 – is profound LOL… She's BRILLIANT!) I'm so sad that you're not here to tell her how proud of her you are, because I KNOW how proud of her you are, but she never got to know you the way that she should have, and now I have to end this letter because I am near tears…

I love you every day. The same as yesterday… But, again, I guess you know that, don't you? Well, I didn't get to say it to you enough while you were beside me, so will continue to say it even though now you're not.

Love you,

Stephie

YEAR 2

{ or: the year I tried to hide... until I realized I couldn't }

Something widows are often advised of is that they should put off making any major decisions for a year following the death of their spouse. If I read it once, I read it a hundred times in the stack of grief books that were piled on my nightstand for the better part of two years. And maybe, if you are surrounded by idiots - or vultures - or you take to getting plastered every single day in order to just get through the day (no judgment, but probably not the best condition in which to make big life decisions), or you've never, at any point in your life *ever* had to deal with making a major life decision for yourself or your family (again, no judgment, I realize that many a widow fits into this category), you might want to stick to that one year suggestion. What I learned, however, is that along this journey, as with so many other journeys we will take over the course of our lifetimes, in our attempt to put some sort of sensible framework around seemingly uncontrollable circumstances and emotions to make ourselves feel as if we have some sort of control, we may often give this "one year" rule (among many other "widow rules") precedence over our gut feeling. I found out the hard way that ignoring my intuition would be a costly mistake, both financially and emotionally. While in the throws of early, debilitating grief, indeed our intuition might be a bit bent, but I'd say for the majority of us, it certainly ain't completely broke.

A few months following Ethan's death I had the thought that I would like to sell the home we had purchased only 5 months before he was killed. I had several reasons for this:

- I was saddled with an overwhelming amount of debt that I didn't think I would be able to remain on top of. The amount of money that the house would cost per year just to pay for the mortgage, taxes, and insurance policies would require financial

Life ain't always beautiful, but it's one hell of a ride…

assistance from his family, who had graciously offered said assistance (and for which I was very grateful for). I just didn't want to be a continued burden to them in perpetuity.

- We had purchased that home to raise our family in *together*, and I found it incredibly difficult to continue to do alone in that space what we had planned to do as a couple. And I had the power and ability to change that situation.

- It was a large house that my 2 children and I didn't really need anymore. One might say we probably didn't need it when there were 4 of us anymore than we did when it became 3 of us, however, the entire family and friend dynamic made a big difference while Ethan was alive. It could and would be filled with visiting family and friends and the energy of laughter and good times in a way that ceased when he died. Our home had suddenly become especially and uncomfortably cavernous...

Unfortunately, mine is a cautionary tale of what happens when one does not have life or mortgage insurance. A fact about which I stayed angry at my dead husband for a long, *long* time (and a feeling about which I am fairly ashamed to admit). I can't say with certainty that I would have continued to live in that house had I the ability to pay it off outright, but the money would have definitely alleviated some of my worries at the time, and perhaps made some of the decision making process a bit easier – I would have had more of an ability to make choices based on what I and my girls needed with less emphasis on whether or not it would remove financial stress from myself or anyone else who was helping me along financially, and there were multiple people who were reaching into their pockets to try to help me survive. To this day I find it difficult to express the depths of my gratitude to those who made my business their business. But back to the house thing…

In the end, with the statement "don't make any decisions for one year" ringing in my ears, and against my own better judgment, I decided to wait until I was in that magically better place (you know, in a year) before making a decision about selling the house. Unfortunately my wait was met face-to-face with one of the worst recessions in US history, and the subsequent ~~housing debacle~~ mortgage crisis. I would eventually find myself sitting on a $900,000 house, with a $699.999 price tag, attempting to succeed – and failing dreadfully – as a seller in a serious "buyers market". The fact that I wasn't one of the unfortunate people facing the loss of their home to foreclosure didn't matter in the end. That whole "what the market will bear" thing became a really big pain in my ass – and my bank account, which, without the benefit of my husband's income, was depleting rapidly under the weight of our financial obligations.

So why did I sell when I did? After waiting that long, why didn't I just wait it out a year or two (or three) longer, you ask?

18 months after Ethan's death I found myself being downsized at work. And by downsized, I'm referring basically to my salary, not my actual job, which I could have kept in *some* capacity, at least for a while until my boss would eventually head for better opportunities on the East Coast. So the party would have completely ended at some point anyway. But for me at the time, the salary was the most important part of the equation. Oh, who am I kidding, it was pretty much the *entire* equation. If I was already struggling financially with the salary I was on (which wasn't small), there was no way that I could possibly survive on less. And as I watched my beloved music industry shrink and merge, and fight a losing battle against emerging technology (that would

eventually all but destroy it), I didn't feel confident that I would be able to find another position that would offer me the same financial reward AND be understanding of my "solo parent" status, allowing me some flexibility, which my current job did. I felt the universe was finally forcing me to make a decision, and that decision was that I would pack up, sell off (or perhaps *out*, depending on who you asked), and head south – to start a new chapter in Nashville. Much like the rest of this story, this leg of the journey wouldn't be easy.

Many, many months (nearly a year in fact) on the market, and $200,000 in financial losses later, in 2009 I was finally able to sell our house. It was a pretty painful experience. It wasn't bad enough that my husband was gone and I was slowly having to let go of the dreams we had together, in one last twist of the knife, nearly everything we had invested in order to buy the house was gone as well. In an act of good faith (and their unfaltering support), Ethan's parents had advanced the purchase of the house Nashville in order to help move my *move* along. The plan was they would get paid back with the proceeds from selling the Los Angeles house. I would be nearly completely out of debt, and could focus on my little family's future. I should know better than to think that things work out according to plan, especially not *my* things. I ended up moving 2,000 miles away, still in debt – and even more indebted to the people who had lost as much as I had. It began to feel like a hole that I would never be able to dig myself out of, made all the worse because I'd managed to drag down the people who were selfless enough to actually throw down a rope.

Yeah, year two (and into three) would prove to be challenging on many fronts. As the fog of grief began to lift, the desire, yet emotional inability, to cut loose from all of this weight - a struggle that never seemed to end – seemed to meet with a force I certainly was not prepared for.

* * * *

As I rounded the bend of the 15 month mark, I realized that my attempts to handle my loss on my own were, perhaps, not enough. I'm a pretty tough cookie, and having survived more than my fair share of trials before stumbling into, undoubtedly, my most difficult one, I thought I was well equipped to find my way through it alone. Rarely have I ever been more wrong. I needed help – terribly – and this being before the peer support and widow groups that one might find now on or through social media outlets, with the exception of one online bulletin board (which I thank the stars for to this very day), I was pretty much on my own. But as that oft-mentioned fog began to clear as I journeyed through my second year, I realized that I was really in need of some on the ground, "real life" help with my grief. It was at this point that I decided to try to find a local young widow grief counseling group.

You would think that in a city as large and diverse (and crime riddled) as Los Angeles that finding a widow group for people under the age of eighty-freakin-seven wouldn't be an exceptionally difficult task, and perhaps nowadays it isn't. But in 2008, when I finally found an organization that provided group counseling to young widows, it was like finding a needle in a haystack. After contemplating making the call for a couple of days, I finally decided I had to reach out, so I took the cowardly approach and sent them an email. The relief I felt at having taken the step to help myself – that girl who never needed any help – was short lived. I was shocked and disappointed to receive a message back from them informing me that they could not accept me into their group counseling program because I was 15 months out from my loss – and their cutoff was 14 months.

I was being shunned by a widow group for being one month too far out from my husband's death.

Okay, perhaps shunned is a little dramatic, but that is essentially how I felt. I was astounded that an organization created to help grieving widows could know so little about grief and loss. The idea of dismissing widows after 14 months because they should somehow be better, or fine, or in some magically different "place" is utterly ridiculous. I was relatively new to the journey, but even then I felt that it seemed unwise (dare I say ignorant) to categorize grief in such nice, clean little timeframes. Now, as I sit writing years after my loss, this is a fact that I can say with certainty.

This response sent me into a tailspin. I felt at that point that I was absolutely alone in my grief and I began to feel utterly helpless. Would I ever feel better? Would this pain I felt inside ever stop? Was there something wrong with me because I didn't already feel better, because their response certainly made me feel like perhaps there was. And WHY couldn't anyone answer any of these questions for me?

I was becoming tired of the questions, I just wanted *answers*. And a really long nap…

But if my life had taught me anything throughout all of my years of travel, it was this: you just have to keep going, no matter what.

Walking through the dark can make you feel like you are walking in circles, even when you are not. It's tempting to just stop, to just give up. But if you are courageous enough to just. keep. going… you will eventually find daylight…

10

WITH LIBERTY, AND JUSTICE FOR ALL... WHATEVER...
{ December 9, 2008 }

So today I received an unexpected and quite disturbing letter in the mail. It came from the California department of corrections. The person who killed Ethan is currently comfortably housed at the Men's colony in San Louis Obispo, just off highway one. It's a minimum security facility where he is able to partake in educational and work skills opportunities, get financial advice from the embezzler he is probably sharing a cell with, and enjoy cool ocean breezes. Anyway, I received a letter today that informed me that his earliest possible date of release is 12/08/09.

Wait a minute, that doesn't seem right...

He is supposed to, according to the way the law was explained to me, serve a minimum of 60% of his 6 year sentence. That would be 42 months minimum. How did that get reduced to 26 months?? And how the hell does the state, or anyone else for that matter, think that 24 months is a suitable amount of time for a murderer???

Let's not even talk about the fact that December 8th is 4 days before Ethan's birthday. I mean the bastard killed my husband the day before our wedding anniversary, and now he's going to possibly be released 4 days before his birthday? Will there be a sacred date left on my calendar?

Life ain't always beautiful, but it's one hell of a ride...

I'm absolutely sick over this. And made all the more rotten because there is f*ck all I can do about it...

11

READY, SET... HANG ON A SEC...
{ December 9, 2008 }

Well, a couple of days ago I returned from Nashville, for what I hope to be the final time that I "fly home to Los Angeles". Now I start the tedious process of attempting to get organized and packed for a cross country move.

Blehhhhh

Anyway, besides the whole "whadya-mean-you-didn't-realize-there-would-be-3-porch-steps-and-they're-going-to-cost-me-an-additional-$1000-or-you're-not-taking-my-stuff-off-the-truck" part of moving, I'm actually looking forward to the adventure of it all.

But for the small issue of still owning my *current* home.

Now, this wasn't part of the plan. The plan was that I would do a loooong escrow in Nashville - which I did - and that would give me the necessary time to sell up here in LA - which, apparently, it didn't.

Now that I've mentioned that, it brings up a really frustrating issue...

The **media.** Now, as a member of the esteemed entertainment industry, I consider the fine people that make the news in all of its forms akin to my second cousins in Kansas City that I've never met. I wouldn't know ya if I passed you on the street, but you're still family. I'm all for you getting along how ever you get along, and feel strongly about the right to free speech,

Life ain't always beautiful, but it's one hell of a ride...

freedom of information, and all of those wonderful liberties we are so fortunate to have. HOWEVER, the media is causing ridiculously unnecessary chaos to the 93% of homeowners that aren't losing their homes (you know, the REST of us that don't get any press...) by blasting the top of the news daily that house prices OOOHHHH and everyone is desperate to sell OOOHHHH and foreclosures OOOHHHH... It just really pisses me off, because you know what happens? People come into neighborhoods that have had a handful of foreclosures/short sales over the last year, which is probably the same number of foreclosures for ANY given year in ANY economic climate, and they expect something for nothing. They think that everyone is losing their ass, so they will just sit and wait until they can get a little more of whatever is left. I mean, don't get me wrong, I'm all about getting a good deal. Yeah, it's common knowledge that I live and die for the Nordstrom half yearly. But seriously, folks, we're not talking about Jimmy Choos, here. Do you know what it takes to keep a house of this kind sparkling clean (with a 3 year old!) for your viewing pleasure?

If my house is out of your price range then take a hike! If you're still waiting for prices to fall, let me know that so I can tell you f*ck off at the threshold because you are truly wasting my time. And if you want something for nothing right now go to Riverside or Lancaster and quit prancin' around here like you actually have some money to spend...

Whew!! Man do I feel better about getting that out!!

Back to more positive stuff...

Regardless of the house situation here, I am determined to keep it movin'. I've gone through a lot over the past two or so years, and it's time for positive change. This is just another bump in the road to happiness, I suppose. More like a big-ass pothole, but who's paying any attention?

So let the fun begin! Though I've missed my goal of NOT ringing in another new year here in Los Angeles, at least I know that this one will be my last, which was something I wasn't sure of this time last year. Actually, come to think of it, this time last year, I wasn't sure what day it was or whether I was coming or going.

So I guess I have truly come a looong way, even if it feels sometimes like I'm standing still...

12

BAH HUMBUG!
{ December 10, 2008 }

So I've decided that I will not get a Christmas tree this year. Now, this is BIG. I am a huge believer in Christmas and all of its trappings, but I just can't be bothered this year.

Sigh...

I will put small trees in the girls' rooms so they can see twinkly lights and all that, but we will have no "big tree" in the living room like we've had pretty much every year of either of their lives. This is due in part to the fact that all of my Christmas ornaments are in storage, but that's not really a hurdle. We all know how I love to shop, and that would just give me a great excuse to have to buy ALL NEW Christmas stuff. But it's really more about the fact that I just don't feel much like celebrating anything this year. I'm just not there yet. I really thought I would be in a better place by now, but I guess I'm just not...

I remember last year going to the lot to buy the tree with my girls. It was the same lot that we'd gone to the previous year to buy the tree. Together. As a family. I remember they had a petting zoo and a Santa. I remember the two of us being so excited about being in our new neighborhood, and just wanting to dive in to all of the local places - yes, including the local Christmas tree lot (which was a pumpkin patch during

Halloween, we'd gotten our pumpkin there that year, too...). We were so excited about the new life we were building in our new home. So last year, without Ethan, I remember crying while at the lot, and weeping as the boys from the lot tied the tree to the top of the car. I'm sure that they thought I was crazy. Or drunk. Or both. Hey, in this town, none of that would be much of a stretch. But, I digress...

     I simply can't put myself through that again this year. And, financially, I'm sure that I can find something better to drop $75 on than a tree that's just going to be a big pain to take down and get rid of anyway once it's all over. I hope that Ethan won't be too disappointed in me, he was such a big kid when it came to the holidays. I do feel like I'm kind of letting everyone down - including him. Maybe I'll feel better next year. Here's to hoping...

13

HAPPY BIRTHDAY, ETHAN
{ December 12, 2008 }

I should be crying, but I just can't let it show.

I should be hoping, but I can't stop thinking
Of all the things we should've said,
That were never said.
All the things we should've done,
That we never did.
All the things that you needed from me.
All the things that you wanted for me.
All the things that I should've given,
But I didn't.

Oh, darling, make it go away.
Just make it go away now.

(Kate Bush, *This Woman's Work*)

Today marks what would have been Ethan's 32nd birthday. On a day that should be filled with happiness, really bad "age" jokes and, more than likely, at least one beer bong (as I sit rolling my eyes), instead I am sitting alone, in *our* bed, pondering what was, what is, and what will never be.

I have to admit, as much as I truly loved my husband, I guess I wasn't always so good at showing it. The life I've lived has left me a bit tough around the edges, and that has a way of creeping into even the most intimate of relationships, and I think that hurt him. Sometimes maybe a great deal.

Ethan, I'm sorry for not being the wife that you deserved. For not giving you, giving us, the absolute best of myself. I hope that somehow you can find a way to forgive me, and that you know how much I really loved you...

"This Woman's Work" written by Kate Bush.
©1988 Sony ATV Music Publishing LLC.

14

FROM THE MOUTHS OF BABES
{ December 13, 2008 }

So yesterday I decided for Ethan's birthday Ava and I would get a dozen balloons and release them at sunset. I thought it might be a nice tradition that the two of us could do each year, now that she's 3 and understands the idea of birthdays, etc. A dozen was the number I chose because his birthday is 12/12. I chose various shades of green latex and mylar (foil) balloons, since green was his favorite color, as well as 2 "happy birthday" balloons.

So we finally make it home, one balloon short (it popped while I was squeezing it into the car...), and it's perfect timing for sunset. Of course, it's also time for the moon rising, and, incidentally, last night happened to be the biggest full moon of the year (yes, there is such a thing...), which I found interesting, and very appropriate (it has something to do with Ethan wanting everyone to GO CRAZY on his birthday, I'm sure...). We walked out to the back yard and go to the outside edge so we have good clearance. I remove the clip and hand the balloons to Ava to do the "honors". Now, I'm thinking that the balloons are going to go away from the house - west - toward the ocean. Up, of course, but at a good angle. Ava lets go of them and they shoot straight up from where we are standing. Literally almost straight up, only slightly over the house (essentially the opposite direction I'd expected them to go) and very quickly are disappearing from site (more quickly than I'd thought as well). The conversation that followed went something like this:

Ava: "Up, up and away!"

Me: "Yes, up, up and away..."

Ava: "They're flying up in the sky"

Me: "Yes, they're flying up in the sky"

Ava: "They're flying up to Dada's house"

Me: (pause.) "Yes they're flying up to Dada's house"

Ava: "Yeah. They can't walk, they have to fly to dada's house"

Me: "That's right...

Now, I've never told her that Daddy lived in the sky. Or that Heaven was in the sky. I've maybe mentioned that Daddy was in heaven twice in two years because I thought that she was too young to really grasp the concept of heaven and the where/why/what-fors of that whole subject, and she was only 1 1/2 when Ethan passed away.

She really knocked me for a loop with that one.

They say that children are more in tune with the earth. They're primal. You know, before we feed them a bunch of malarkey about a bunch of man-made-up stuff. Maybe it's true. Maybe she does know where her Dada is. Maybe it's me with the problem...

Life ain't always beautiful, but it's one hell of a ride...

15

MORE GENIUS FROM THE PROGENY
{ December 16, 2008 }

Ava: Mommy...

Me: Yes, honey?

Ava: You look distinguished

Me: Why, thank you.

The fact that it took the unadulterated wisdom of a 3 year old to recognize the clear truth, well... the truth has been told is all that matters at the end of the day, right?

The fact that this profound statement was followed by the far less profound made up song titled "I don't have any boogies" matters not. I look distinguished. It has been said, and so it is...

16

WITH TEN MILES BEHIND ME, AND TEN THOUSAND MORE TO GO...
{ December 21, 2008 }

Necessity is the mother of invention.

Then laziness, I suppose, would be the mother of shortcuts...

I have managed to import all of my blog posts from my former blogger blog (which is quite dusty these days) into this shiny, new and improved blog, with the simple touch of a button. Technology, I take back all the nasty things I've said about you! If you can keep your eyes open long enough, and you're new to my blog/situation, it might provide interesting reading, or at least a good glimpse as to what brought me to where I am now. If you've already read my former blog, I'm so sorry to bore you LOL...

I started to read back over my old posts, starting with the very first. Those are thoughts I hadn't had in a while, and it was a difficult read. Although I was several months out from losing Ethan at the time, the wounds were very, very fresh. Reading those words again tonight was akin to re-scraping the same nasty scrape that had managed to scab over. However, unlike, say, 6 or 8 months ago, new scar tissue has begun to grow, and the wound is unable to be opened to the same extent. For that I am grateful, and I must say, surprised. You never, ever think you will get to a place where simple words like "accident", "coroner", "buried" (used in just about any

Life ain't always beautiful, but it's one hell of a ride...

context) would not cause you to completely lose it. I am glad to say that, apparently, I have traveled some way down this very solitary road. I know I have a long way to go, but as I look back I can say I am satisfied by the miles I've managed to put behind me...

BTW, you'll notice that the title of this post is a song lyric. In my old posts you'll see that almost all the titles are lyrics, it was my way of putting another part of myself into my blogs. The overall song may not necessarily have to do with the blog post, but, just, perhaps that one line struck a chord in relation to what I was writing about. I actually really like the challenge of racking my brain for a long lost lyric and coming up with something that made sense, and have decided, starting with this post, that I will go back to the practice.

Double points for those of you who can figure out the songs the titles are culled from. No googling, of course...

17

O' TANNENBAUM, O' TANNENBAUM
{ December 22, 2008 }

Sigh...

So, despite my objections, there is now a Christmas tree in my family room. It's a small tree. Not as small as I'd planned, however, I guess I waited too long to buy one to have my "pick of the litter" and took what I could get. This after going to 3 places in the cold and wet, and finally ending up at the dreaded lot that we've always bought our trees that I'd been attempting to avoid like the plague. And, just like last year, I bawled like a baby while sitting in my car after finally finding a tree and getting them to cut the price by $30 (yeah, they tried to charge me $60 for a 4ft douglas fur, it's sick, really). Must have been Mariah ad-libbing "sleep in Heavenly peeeeeeaaaaaace" over and over and OVER. I just finally lost it...

Anywho... Unfortunately, because all of my ornaments are in storage, and I'd only bought a few, small scaled ornaments for a small tree I'd planned to put in my bedroom, the tree looks, well, kind of odd. It's kind of like a really big guy wearing a t-shirt 3 sizes too small LOL. Oh well, at this point, I'm not spending a penny more on this holiday, so it'll have to do...

A couple of things that are very different about this tree, from trees past:

a) It's small. Ethan and I didn't allow the words "small" "Christmas" and "tree" to be used in succession in a sentence. We always got the largest tree we could squeeze into the room. Our first place together had massive vaulted ceilings. It took 4 grown men to get that tree into the house, but it was fabulous! This tree is on an overturned cardboard box covered with a tablecloth, and it still looks small...

b) It's in the family room. Between the breakfast table and the couch. As opposed to the regal position in the formal living room, I just wanted to downplay the whole "very special holiday-ness" of the whole thing. If I had my way, I would just crawl under a rock until, oh, January 7th or so. But, I don't think that would be fair to the girls, so...

c) I let the girls decorate it. Other than putting on the lights and some ribbon (as garland), I pretty much let the girls do it. This is a MAJOR change from the control-freak-scary-obsessive way in which I usually decorate for Christmas (or any other time for that matter). In fact, all 15 of the gold mini pears Ava put along the bottom-most branches of the tree are all still in their same place, and there they will remain, until some point after Christmas when we take it all down and get back to our regularly scheduled lives, for whatever that's worth.

So now there is a proper place for Santa to drop of the (few) gifts when he manages to squish his fat ass down the chimney. Hopefully I won't still be up with a Vanilla Stoli and Coke in my hand watching Roseanne or something. Lord knows how I HATE to be interrupted while watching Roseanne...

Repeat after me: Bah Humbug.

There is *one* thing about this tree that is similar to last year's tree. On it hangs the wonderful memorial angel ornament I was given to commemorate

Ethan's life. It's hanging in its rightful place, on the uppermost branch in the front of the tree.

I really miss you baby...

18

ALL'S I GOT IS TIME.
GOT NO MEANING, JUST A RHYME
{ December 24, 2008 }

The insomnia is back. And she's got me by the throat. December is a hard month for most of us that have lost loved ones. The month is compounded by Ethan's birthday, so the neurosis starts fairly early for me and flows right on through the New Year. Yay me.

The nights are loooong these days. I'm a good two weeks into this... this... *moment.* Watching the clock - 3AM... 4:27... 5:06... 6:10 - Watching the morning creep upon the night. I can roll down the best late night tv lineup on Directv for pretty much every night of the week by rote. Unfortunately, tonight is presenting me with a dilemma as many of the cable networks have changed their schedules because of the holiday. From 3-4AM tonight, two of the best 3 selections are "Jessica Simpson Uses Pro-Active" and "Is Colon Detox Hype?" Deciding both of those are pretty much the very same infomercial, I've chosen to punish myself with an hour long program about how they now think Egypt is older than they previously thought. If that doesn't break the sleepless cycle, NOTHING will.

Oh, not quite making the top 3 were reruns of Full House. Yes, I would rather listen to someone discussing the benefits of cleaning out my ass than be subject to 30 minutes of full house...

Well, I guess I'll be getting back to my graham crackers and Limonata and settle in for another long night of 3rd rate entertainment. Sigh....

19

DECEMBER WILL BE MAGIC AGAIN
{ December 25, 2008 }

Today was, as expected, bittersweet. I think that I did pretty good, all things considered. There were several times today that the 'ole eyes began to well up, but I didn't fall apart, and for that I am very pleased...

So now, after a very scaled back morning of gift unwrapping, and afternoon sitting around gorging on the 11 tons of cookies I baked and a very casual Christmas dinner, the youngest is in bed having sweet dreams, I'm sure, and the big one is in the living room occasionally peeking up from the new iPod Touch. I've excused myself, oddly, to the living room...

This is odd because, well, I've not sat in here but one other time in the two years we've lived in the house. That one other time was when Ethan died. I remember sitting on my brand new (at the time) couches and talking to some stranger from the victim services department who had come to my home to give me information to help me deal with some of the legal nonsense that I would be dealing with from what had happened. I couldn't tell you one single word he said to me, actually, as I rack my brain trying to come up with some portion of that conversation. But I remember it would be nearly another two years before I sat in this room, on this couch.

Tonight I've lit a fire - the first time since living in the house, which is ridiculous since it's gas for cryin' out loud. Turn the key light the long lighter thingy. Simple dimple. Just never did it. So I'm sitting here, in the dim, quiet room, looking out of the picture window in the front of the house to the house across the street, which I'm sure is responsible for Santa finding our house from the outer hemisphere AND for that power surge we had last night. It sure is pretty though. And if Ethan were here, ours would look like that, only a bit more low-brow because I'm sure he'd have bought every last animatronic multi-colored light thing in four counties to stick on our little patch of front lawn.

But, he's not here, so there are no lights. But I have hope that someday, maybe in a year not too far from now, I will find the Christmas spirit once again. My home will glow inside and out with decked halls and holiday cheer. We will carol. We will bake. We will celebrate like it's 1999. Someday. But for now, I will settle for happy children and the warm glow of my "very first fire", and the guts to not have completely thrown in the towel on the whole thing...

Merry Christmas, and much peace, to all...

20

MY EYES ARE GREEN
'CAUSE I EAT A LOT OF VEGETABLES...
{ December 28, 2008 }

For obvious reasons, the loss of a spouse can really bring out the worst in us. Sometimes it brings out things we didn't even know existed within ourselves. The normal processes of living, being carried out by others, can often become incredibly difficult situations for those of us that are still in the throes of grief.

What I speak of here, friends, is envy. One of the Cardinal Sins, if you will. Not jealousy, but **envy**. What's the difference you ask? Well, everyone harbors a bit of jealousy - the desire to have something that someone else possess. Envy, however, is *resenting someone for having something you lack, and wanting that other person to be deprived of whatever it is.* A whole different level of play. Pretty serious stuff when you really think about it. What would bring on such negative feelings? Well, I'll explain as best I can...

There are the everyday things one can't help but see and/or experience: couples holding hands; children happily riding upon the shoulders of their loving, strong daddies; couples shopping together, laughing. I feel a sense of jealousy for all of that, which, I think is natural, and not unique to just the grieving widow. A girl who's broken up with her boyfriend would probably

Life ain't always beautiful, but it's one hell of a ride...

share my feelings of all that everyday kind of stuff. I want that, but don't wish for those who do have those things to no longer have them.

But, then we get into the more difficult things - baby showers, giving birth, weddings, those sorts of things. Those trigger a whole different level of emotion to me. I not only feel jealousy, but I get that *"Why do YOU get all this? All this love? All this happiness? You don't deserve it anymore than me, and I don't think it's fair that YOU get it. I wish YOU had it all snatched away from you, I wish you could feel my pain for just 1 hour. I wish that you had to know what it felt like to have a child who has no recollection of the amazing father she had before some idiot took his life"* feeling...

Now, for the record, I wouldn't wish what I've gone through, what I go through on a regular basis, on my worst enemy. Honestly, I wouldn't. But there are just times when this envy takes over me, and I feel such anger for the fact that Ethan and I and our families were chosen for this. I mean, this doesn't happen to *us.* This happens to people on tv. To *them.* When I feel this way, I just want to crawl under a rock, because I know darn well that it's not the subject of my envy's fault that this has happened to us, I DO realize that. However, they become the sole focus of my negative emotions. Some people might call this displaced anger. Trust me when I say it's not. I have a lot of anger, and it's very clearly manifested itself in all kinds of strange ways and at the most inopportune moments. Yelling at unsuspecting store clerks for not having a gift box - that's displaced anger. Driving with my hand on my horn for 3/4 of mile because someone cut me off - that's displaced anger.

This ain't *that.*

This is a feeling altogether separate. I think they are such highly emotionally charged events that they push everyone's emotions to their absolute peak. I mean, I've always been the type that will cry at a fake wedding on tv. I just get so into the words that they affect me on a very deep level (I know, sounds ridiculous). So what may have been a bit of jealousy under normal circumstances, spills over into envy territory when it comes to the major life events.

When all of your senses are already heightened, I guess what is created is a very fine line. When I'm not careful I trip and fall over that line...

Dante would have my green eyes sewn shut with wire. Thank God I live in 2008 (and in real life, such as it is) where my punishment is just having to live with my own shame. Then again, I'm not sure which is truly worse when you know something you're feeling is so wrong....

21

TURN THE CLOCK TO ZERO, MACK
{ December 31, 2008 }

So, a few days ago, before Christmas, my girls and I were - like so many of you - plodding around the local mall. Mostly people watching, it was simply a way of getting out of the house. We decided to stop for lunch at the very snazzy food court in this particular mall (you eat on REAL plates with REAL knives and forks... even if you're just eating chicken nuggets!), and our vendor... or, uh... "restaurant" of choice was Panda Express.

Okay, so it's not the most authentic Chinese food around, but the 14 year old loves it, and it was Christmas, after all, so I decided to indulge her.

In usual American Chinese restaurant fashion, we each received a fortune cookie with our meal. The girls ate theirs. I saved mine. Two nights ago after posting my video blog about the new year, resolutions, yadda yadda, I was feeling peckish so I started scrounging around the kitchen for a snack. I ended up with a delightful smorgasbord of marshmallows, salt and pepper potato chips - and one fortune cookie.

I cracked it open, pulled out the scroll, took the requisite bite from the cookie and read my "fortune". I smiled as I read:

DON'T LOOK BACK,
ALWAYS LOOK AHEAD
PANDA EXPRESS • PANDA INN

So. There ya have it. Ancient wisdom? Fluke-y generic pre-printed nonsense? Tactical positioning on the part of the Fates? Who knows. But I had to consider the timing (and no, neither of the girls got the same "new year themed" fortune in theirs), and take it under advisement.

It's good advice, no matter where it comes from, I think. And I think it's high time I start spending less time looking back and more time looking ahead.

So here's to looking ahead at the opportunity of a new year. Looking ahead with hope. Looking ahead with positivity.

Peace to you all...

Life ain't always beautiful, but it's one hell of a ride...

ROUGH ROAD

YEAR 3

{ or: that year I finally got tired of getting knocked around by grief}

Grief has no timeline. The concept of the oft referenced "5 stages of grief" is a feeble attempt to give a nice, clean, linear timeline to a chaotic, uncontrollable, and sometimes frightening emotional rollercoaster, in order to assuage the uncomfortable idea of being psychologically and/or emotionally out of control, which grief can certainly make you feel. The *"5 stages"*, however, was never intended to be attributed to those who were grieving the loss of a loved one, rather, it was developed from a study of terminally ill patients who were facing the end of their own lives, as they processed the reality of their own mortality. And while this is fairly well known throughout the mental health community, there are still many "experts", including many in the medical community at large, but certainly includes folks who write articles on and off-line and appear in the media who cling to, and continue to perpetuate, this misappropriated grief theory. This allows it to remain in our vernacular, ready to annoy grievers when it is waved in our face by well meaning friends and family who, because of this "5 stage" theory, think they know where you should be, how you should be behaving, and how or what you should be feeling.

You know: whether or not you're grieving right.

 But, man! Wouldn't it be nice? To just be able to go down the aisle, marking off the phases of your grief as you experience them, like a grocery shopping list, or checking off the boxes one by one, like you were packing for a summer vay-cay?

Okay, denial… done it, toss it in the suitcase.

Anger? Oh, yep, there you are. All done, chuck it in the bag.

Bargaining? Boy… yep… did some-a-you! Get on in that suitcase!

Depression? Sooo done. In the bag you go.

Life ain't always beautiful, but it's one hell of a ride…

Ahhh, yes, acceptance. Finally! You come with me. We shall go hand in hand to live happily ever after…

Once you've collected all five of your little "stages" in your nice little suitcase (with the exception of acceptance, which you've safely tucked in your pocket), stick a tag on it directing it to Timbuktu (*Hey, grief! SEE YAAA!).*

Well, it doesn't work like that. And anyone who tries to tell you that it does, or tries to connect what you are feeling with some sort of nice, neat "stage" of grief, healing, or *whatever,* is someone who is fortunate enough to have either never had the occasion to suffer significant loss, or seriously just lives in LaLa Land. If you're reading this because you have had the unfortunate occasion to lose your love, well then, you understand that either of those scenarios would be much preferred to where you likely are.

Lucky them, right? As for the rest of us…

There are no clear and neat phases, stages, or categories one can really use to present an organized structure for grief and healing, no matter who tries to establish one (and many have come up with various, lesser known "stage" based theories). I've always said that grief is as individual to us as our fingerprints; each one of us will journey through our own grief in our very own unique way. However, what I will say at this point with quite a bit of certainty is that there are some things that grieving widow(er)s experience that I would venture to say are *not particularly uncommon.*

The "first year fog" seems to be a very common experience, followed by the feeling of suddenly having the rug ripped out from under you all over again as you venture through the second year, and that grief fog begins to clear. And by common, I certainly don't mean to insinuate that it happens to *everyone,* it is just something in my personal experience, followed by years of connection and observation of other widow(er)s, that seems to be an oft

Life ain't always beautiful, but it's one hell of a ride…

expressed occurrence. It certainly was something I experienced. Getting through those first two years seemed like one long game of *grief whack-a-mole*; no sooner had I whacked an emotion, it popped right back up *over there* to taunt me, usually bringing along a few new friends. I spent two years whackin' away at a bunch of feelings and emotions I didn't always understand, just for them to pop back up later to surprise me. All I really feel I got out of it was complete exhaustion. But then it all took an interesting turn in my 3rd year: with the fog totally subsided I could finally see that there were more things to do than just hanging out, whacking at tenacious little *grief moles*. After all, since they were just going to continue to pop up anyway, perhaps my time might be better spent focused on some other, more productive activities.

Year 3, for me, would be the year of massive physical and emotional transition, and the year that I realized there might be life out there beyond the *valley of the moles*…

* * * *

While I like to believe I did a good job of remaining ever mindful of the fact that I was not the only one who had suffered an incredible loss when my husband died, it was in my third year that I really began to see a bigger picture emerge in terms of not only our shared loss, but the healing journeys of the many close family members and friends who also loved Ethan and also missed him dearly. I realized that because he was my husband and prior to his death every aspect of my life included him, thus I was directly impacted each and every day with the fact that he was absent. Having said that, I still can't fathom what his parents must have felt in those early months and years, as no matter how far away they are, or how often you might see them, losing your child – at any age – is simply unimaginable to me. And I thought often of

Life ain't always beautiful, but it's one hell of a ride…

his several close friends from his hometown, who he continued to stay tightly connected to even after everyone went their separate ways as adults. Living so far away from them all, though we spoke on occasion, I saw them rarely, so I did not bear direct witness to their personal grief and their journey to heal from the loss of their beloved friend. It was always a bit strange to me when I experienced our relationships within this new dynamic – relationships that were now being forged between them and me directly, with no *middle man*.

I realize that I am among the lucky. There are many widow(er)s who lose their partner's side of the family and/or those friends their partner brought to their relationship, once the *middle man* has passed away. The reasons this happens are many and varied, however, whenever I hear of such experiences it always makes me sad, while at the very same time, incredibly grateful. Death and grief can really bring out the worst in people, but just as a coin has two sides, I've seen it bring out the absolute best in people as well. In my case there seemed to be a mutual respect for all involved, coupled with what felt like a collective need to protect each other. Maybe I'm just imagining that, but that is how it felt, so I'm going to go with it. No one ever told me I was *doing it all wrong*, instead they quietly allowed me to process through my *process*, as they all quietly processed through theirs.

Occasionally some of us would gather and *process* together. It was on one such occasion toward the end of this particular year of my journey that would shine a light on the fact that we were, indeed, tightly bound together by a shared experience – one that was offering us all an opportunity to emotionally evolve. One winter evening when I was visiting my in-laws, I went out to the local dive for a drink with a few of Ethan's life-long friends. While I always enjoyed the opportunity to connect with them, I was always a little unsure about how they felt about me. Ethan and I hadn't been married long

Life ain't always beautiful, but it's one hell of a ride...

when he died, and we (gasp!) didn't have a perfect marriage, which always left me wondering what thoughts or feelings Ethan might have had that I wasn't aware of – thoughts and feelings that has his friends they may have been privy to. Did they think I was a terrible wife to their friend? Did they at all blame me in some way for Ethan's death? As silly as these questions may seem, and as redundant as they may have been at that point, to me (at the time) they felt valid because I suffered such guilt in the years after he died, blaming myself for so many things – every once in a while *those things* would include his death. It made total sense to me that, right or wrong, others who loved him might hold me accountable for his death in some way as well.

But on this night, one brief conversation would help clarify how they felt about me, in relation to our shared loss, and our new – direct - relationship.

As we sat in that smoky little bar, getting caught up, sharing stories about Ethan (but without Ethan, which was still a little weird then), one of his closest friends turned to me and said: "Can I ask you something? You don't have to answer me if you don't want to."

Now, in my experience whenever anyone buffers a question with "you don't have to answer it if you don't want to," it's generally a sign that something embarrassing, or at the very least uncomfortable, is coming down the pipe. And this instance would prove to be no different. Of course I gave the only response one can in such situations: "sure, okay…" although inside I was thinking: "uh oh…"

And that's when he asked me the dreaded question. One that I had hoped to avoid at all costs for… well… for*ever.*

"Are you, like, dating… anyone… at all?"

Oh. Shit.

Here I was sitting in *his* town, with *his* friends, and *he's not here* – it's just little ol' me, his wife – I was still his wife, right? And his buddies wanted to know if I was dating? I had absolutely no idea what the right answer was supposed to be to this very tricky question. Was I supposed to be dating – or was I expected to remain alone forever, carrying a brightly burning torch for my one and only love – their amazing and beautiful, but dead friend? If I was dating, were they going to pull the welcome mat from under my feet? What about Ava? I was relying on these men – Ethan's closest friends – to be a part of Ava's life, to help guide her and to fill inevitable voids with stories of her father that only they could tell. Was all of that now in jeopardy?

Truth is, I had… *dabbled.* I wasn't sure up until then that I was ready to call it *dating,* per se. And, yes, there is a difference between dabbling and dating. Going on a blind date… or two (hey, everybody's gotta eat, might as well do it with a total stranger while navigating awkward conversation): *dabbling.* The one or two guys that you have handy in case you need a party/wedding/event escort: *dabbling.* Wearing matching "I'm with stupid" t-shirts on your weekend getaway: *dating.* Going together to his kid's first grade play: *dating.* Heck, meeting their kids (or his mother), at all: *dating.* You get the idea now...

I'm not sure I was ready to call whatever I was doing with, uh, whomever I was doing it with, *dating* mostly because I wasn't sure I was emotionally ready *to date.* For so long the idea of being with any other man made me feel like I was cheating on Ethan. I was his widow, which for a long time translated (to me) to "I was still his wife". He was a man who had already been snatched away from this world much too soon, for me to get involved in *dating* another man would just be a betrayal that would essentially be adding insult to injury. Or so I thought for a very long time.

This question had indeed come at an interesting time for me because I had been really struggling with this particular aspect of my journey. Afraid to move forward in case it would be seen (or felt) as a betrayal to my late husband, and definitely afraid to talk to anyone about the possibility, or my struggle with it, in case it would hurt those who loved him so much.

They couldn't find another Ethan, was it fair that I could find another partner to take Ethan's place in my life?

And this is what grief does. Fills your already confused little brain with silly nonsense. And it was all silly, really. It's true: I could find another partner, but I could never *replace* Ethan. Nor would I ever wish to. He was a beautiful man, with a heart of gold and a smile as bright as the sun. He was perfect in his "Ethan-ness", and he left behind impossibly large shoes to fill. Any other man to come into my life worthy of becoming my partner would be loved "in addition to", not "instead of". I think that we widow(er)s can get lost in this issue, not fully realizing how big our hearts really are. We sometimes have trouble grasping the idea that we can carry the love for our late spouse, while nurturing love for a new partner – much in the same way we can love our children equally. We are not required to discard one to make room for the other. It often takes us some time to learn this truth about love after loss. No one else would take away from, or diminish, what Ethan and I had, or the gifts that he gave to me during our time together. If I had to do it all over again, even knowing it would result in the same outcome, I wouldn't hesitate for a second to jump right in with both feet. To have him just for a moment was worth all of the hurt, for the gifts and the many lessons that I received as a result of having loved him are many and profound.

So, I took a breath and with a slightly nervous smile, I replied, "Yeah, I have... *dated.* I've gone on... dates." I let it out and let it ride.

Life ain't always beautiful, but it's one hell of a ride...

He looked at me and smiled, and said, "good. That's good. You should!"

Inside I breathed a massive sigh of relief. In reality, there was never a right or wrong answer, there was only the truth. My husband had been gone for nearly 3 years by then, and it was only natural that at some point I might want to seek some sort of companionship. Whether I chose to date or dabble (or any combination of the two), my husband's death should not (and did not) mark the end of my life as well. I was fortunate to be surrounded by people who loved me enough to understand and accept that fact. And while I had to make the personal choices that worked for me regardless of what other people thought of those choices, their support certainly helped make it easier for me to better understand my own feelings, and embrace my freedom to date... or dabble... if I so chose.

At this point in all of our individual journeys we were each beginning to come to terms with our own loss. This was allowing us a wider perspective, enabling us to see how that loss, and our relationships with one another, would continue to fit into and shape our lives going forward.

Because all of our lives would continue to move forward, and our *middle man* was not coming back...

22

I GRAB MY KEYS AND A BEER
{ January 5, 2009 }

[This post refers to the 60 minutes episode titled "The Case For Murder" which aired on January 4, 2009 it can be found online at:
https://youtu.be/vuac5zZ1gqk
In the episode reporter Bob Simon investigates the growing number of U.S. prosecutors pursuing harsher penalties for drunk drivers, including long prison terms for those who caused fatalities. Among them, Kathleen Rice, District Attorney for Nassau County, NY. She is profiled here, along with a landmark case involving a family whose limousine was hit head on by a wrong-way drunk driver (who had been drinking at a party at a friend's house), resulting in the deaths of both the limo driver as well as 7 year old Katy Flynn. The terrible incident was recorded in full by a dashcam installed in the limo. In the piece, the family – who all suffered major life threatening injuries in the collision – recounts the horrifying details of little Katy's death. The drunk driver who caused the deaths was charged not with the typical lightweight "vehicular manslaughter", but rather, with "murder by depraved indifference" in an attempt to set a new precedent for drunk driving deaths, taking them out of the category of "accident" and placing them, rightfully, in the category "violent crime".]

If you didn't see this 60 Minutes broadcast, please watch it. Please note that it contains some disturbing images/descriptives.

What an overwhelming tragedy. Unfortunately, it's more common than anyone wants to admit.

Life ain't always beautiful, but it's one hell of a ride...

We send money all over the world to fight injustices in other countries, yet everyday we are left with the injustice of our own current drunk driving laws, watered down penalties, designed to coddle murderers. Those who choose to get drunk and operate a vehicle tell us by their actions they have absolutely no regard for human life. Nonetheless, the current system leaves victims shattered, and after being repeatedly disregarded, ultimately their loss is tossed aside in favor of the *rights* of those that caused us to become victims in the first place.

Up till now I've done well to not climb up on my soapbox about this issue here on this blog, and I think I'll scurry down now before I pass the point of no return...

The one thing that has stayed with me from viewing this (aside from the obvious), is I finally know what Ethan saw in the last few moments of his life. The accident was almost identical from a logistical standpoint. Only my husband was in a Honda, not a great big limousine. I've had many, many nightmares about what he may have seen.

And now... I know.

I don't know if that makes me feel better or not...

Please watch. Please discuss. Please take action.

Life ain't always beautiful, but it's one hell of a ride...

23

NOW YOU'RE STUCK IN A MOMENT, AND YOU CAN'T GET OUT OF IT
{ January 8, 2009 }

A couple of weeks ago I was feeling pretty good and I decided that I would get a head start on the packing (oohhh all the packing!) that needs to be done for the move to Nashville. I thought I would start small. A few decorative items that I really don't need, may as well box 'em up, right?

I dragged all of my vases and candleholders and various sentimental glass objects out of cabinets, the garage, or took them off of wherever they had been displayed (good to scale down the "personal stuff" anyway since the house is - *still* - on the market) and brought them into the living room. Got some boxes, pulled out the bubble wrap (you mean everyone doesn't keep reams of bubble wrap on hand? Oh...), and the brown paper. Put it all in the middle of the living room floor. And then I stopped.

And sat. And stared.

And then I walked away.

That was over two weeks ago. The stuff, along with the bubble wrap and boxes, is all still there. Just sitting there, staring at me. I said everyday over the Christmas break "I'm gonna get in there and pack up that stuff". Told

Life ain't always beautiful, but it's one hell of a ride...

my oldest, "today I want you to help me get in there and pack up that stuff". Something is just keeping me from doing it. And, no it's not just laziness, it's like some greater force is rendering me unable to go in there and pack up those couple of vases, nick-knacks and what-nots. I'm beginning to think it has something to do with the **reality** of what's going on. I mean, I know that the house has been on the market for several months, and that people have come and gone and at any time one of those people could have made an offer and the house could have been sold.

But that hasn't been the case.

And I know that I've bought the house in Nashville already and, obviously at some point, the transition would have to be made. But it was always at some point in the *future*.

Now that I have tried to take a step toward really making that transition - by packing up a couple of boxes - I'm finding myself absolutely paralyzed. It's not fear, nor regret, nor uncertainty. And, no, it's not guilt. It's a quiet, yet overwhelming sadness at the fact that I am trying to move into a new phase in my life. And by doing so, I'm leaving behind the "phase" where I was married to Ethan and we had a nice family, home, and life. I am overwhelmingly sad about what has become our reality. I've not really had to think about that so much in many months, or even the better part of the past year. Yeah, it comes up from time to time, and I do shed tears over it. But it's just stuff in my head. I can resolve to "turn it off", but I can't do so with this move. It's physical, there is no "turning it off". It must be faced.

I know that I can't bring back the past. I can not change what happened. I've reconciled myself with that fact, which gave me the strength to make the initial choice to move in the first place. And I know I've even talked about the fact that our memories aren't contained in "things", that our memories are in our hearts and in our minds and they will always be with us, as long as we choose for them to be.

I'm just having a real hard time putting my own words into action. I have to admit that I'm actually having a hard time while even writing about this (I've had to back away from the keyboard a couple of times already)...

I have fallen into a really bad "moment", and I can't seem to get out of it...

I can't sleep. When I finally get to sleep, I can't wake up. The house has fallen into a bit of disarray (okay, it's not that bad, but definitely not in a state for showing). I look like crap. I feel even worse.

And then, there's the pile of stuff on the living room floor.

Maybe having gotten all of this out, I've made the first step in actually working through it. If there is one thing I've learned from all of this, it's that there is really no such thing as "getting over" things. I find much of life, essentially, to be a series of exercises on "working through" things. I really need to work through this. Not now, but RIGHT NOW.

I think I'll start by actually picking up the phone and scheduling those moving companies. Then I will go have a rendezvous with the pile of stuff on the floor in my living room. Now that I know that *someone else knows* I need to get it done, perhaps I will actually... get it done...

24

A FEW MORE WORDS
FROM THE MOUTHS OF BABES
{ January 10, 2009 }

Yesterday my youngest and I were sitting in my office. I was clip-clapping away on my computer, she was sitting across from me (I have an "L" shaped desk) doodling on a piece of paper. Out of the blue she stopped drawing, looked up and addressed me:

Ava: Mommy

Me: Yes...

Ava: Daddy loves you.

...Long pause. I cock my head to one side and ponder this statement...

Me: He does?

Ava: Yes. He loves you really, really much!

Me: He does?

Ava: Yes. And he loves me too!

Now, we probably don't talk about her dad as much as we should, but she's just *so* young, I don't really know what to say to her about it, other than showing her pictures and that sort of thing now and then when the occasion arises. I guess what is so surprising about this is how random it was. We'd

Life ain't always beautiful, but it's one hell of a ride...

not been looking at photos, or talking about him. We were in my office and there aren't any family photos in there, and I don't have a photo of him on my computer screen or anything.

She just knows. And felt she needed to let me know.

This is so hard. You've no idea how hard it is to look at your three year old, and see her fathers face. Her father that she can't possibly have any recollection of. And she finds it appropriate, in her own baby way, to comfort *me* (whether she knew it or not).

Ashamedly, we'd not talked about him directly in a little while. Maybe this was her way of letting me know that it was okay to do so...

Life ain't always beautiful, but it's one hell of a ride...

25

RUNNIN' DOWN THE ROAD
TRYING TO LOOSEN MY LOAD
{ January 15, 2009 }

As I ramble toward the two year anniversary of Ethan's death, I find that I am really beginning to come to certain realizations about my loss, myself, my future. As I turn and look behind me, I am often amazed by what I see. Miles I never thought I would survive. What was once cracked, broken, potholed road for as long as the eye could see, has given way to miles of smoother pavement, with the odd short stretches of bumpy asphalt - to be expected on any journey as long as this - but they become fewer and further between as I continue rolling along...

So many changes happening to me and my family right now, so much to try to grasp, sometimes it feels like I can't cling tight to any of it without it all just falling through my too-narrow fingers. I know that I need to focus on one thing at a time, something that's always been a problem for me (I'm a multi-tasker), but necessary in light of the highly emotionally charged nature of all that is currently happening. So I will stop and I will deal with one task at a time. First on the list: Getting through the move.

I think that Ethan would be proud of my progress. I wish that he didn't have to be, at least not my progress with *this*, anyway. I wish that he could be proud of my progress in my career, or with the children, but since he is not here, I hope that he is proud of my progress on the journey I am now on without him, and my path toward healing.

The journey is complex, trying, sorrowful, *profound*, mind blowing... immensely clarifying. But I believe that there is light at some point along the way (I will not say "the end" because I do not believe any such place exists). I've gained clarity on a lot of issues, both those that matter immensely, and those that do not matter in the least, and I've gown exponentially because of this. I've learned things I never knew I'd want *or need* to learn in my lifetime.

I've been spending a lot of time these past few days pondering those things. Would I have learned them had I not lost Ethan? Would the answer to that even matter had I not lost Ethan? I don't know the answer to that (I sure wish I did), however, I do know that what I have learned is worth sharing. A taster-spoon size helping of so very many things I've learned along the way:

- Healing from this kind of catastrophic loss is a lifetime journey. It DOES get easier, but it IS *forever.*
- There is no such thing as "closure" on matters such as these, nor would I want to "close" the door on what we had, who he was, who *we* were.
- You do not "get over it" you learn to live with it. Like a massive load, you learn just how to carry it "just right" so it doesn't make you topple over under its weight.
- Hind sight is 20/20.
- You can not undo what has been done. He's not coming back. ***Ever.***
- Eating is not a luxury, it's a survival skill.

Life ain't always beautiful, but it's one hell of a ride...

- As much as I'd like to be, I am neither now, nor will I ever be, in control of the entire Universe.
- I **DO** need people after all.
- Kindness is ~~the~~ *an important* key to healing. Be kind to yourself (and others).
- Through the greatest trials, we are offered the greatest opportunities to learn.
- By helping others to heal, you, in turn, help yourself to do the same.
- One is truly the loneliest number.

26

EMANCIPATE YOURSELF FROM MENTAL SLAVERY
{ January 24, 2009 }

I can't believe how many days have gone by since my last post! Hold on, folks, it's gonna be a rambler...

I've gotten very caught up in the whole inaugural thing. I don't think I've watched as much CNN in the past year as I've watched in the past couple of weeks. It's an exciting time for our country, I sure wish Ethan were here to see it. I'm sure that wherever he is, he is very pleased indeed...

Watching the inauguration itself - the throngs of people, the generations of families who showed up to watch this incredible moment of American history - I began to think of my parents, my father in particular, and then his parents. I wondered what they would have thought about all of it had they lived long enough to see this moment.

My Grandparents drove from Louisiana to California during the 1940s in the hopes of escaping segregation and finding a better life for their family. My grandmother was born and raised on a farm in a rural area of northern Louisiana. When I see pictures of the time I can't imagine what they raised there, it just looks to me like a bunch of dried up dirt. As a black woman in Louisiana during the early part of the century, she was not entitled to an education and I remember as a young girl finding out that the only words my Grandmother knew how to actually write were the words contained in her own name. She was married off and had her first child somewhere around the age of 15.

Then I thought about HER grandparents... born into slavery. And I suddenly realized something. I realized that despite my incredible heartache, despite my seemingly overwhelming loss, in "the grand scheme of life", as they say

Perhaps my current struggles aren't that incredibly difficult.

My grandmother had 9 children (including two sets of twins back to back) and, eventually came to raise them all in an apartment in the projects of San Pedro. She was abandoned by my Grandfather for about 10 years (another story for another post), so to feed her family she washed and ironed people's clothes. Yet, I can not recall her ever having a bad thing to say about her life (nor my Grandfather, or any other human for that matter). She came from a very hard place, full of poverty, illness and oppression, backwards laws and even more backward law enforcers, but she always had an open door and a hot meal for anyone who happened by.

I imagined her grandparents, born slaves in the deep (deep!) south. What must it be like to have a baby and have it snatched away, sold, traded as property? To be separated from your parents as a child? Separated from your husband (if your marriage was even acknowledged), brother, sister, or wife? How does it feel to be considered less than a whole person?

I had started, not long ago, to do some ancestry research and of course, like so many others of African American heritage, ran into the "1860 wall", where (in going backwards through generations) documentation of blacks transitions from the birth certificate/marriage records, to finding descriptions of human slaves within itemized real estate transactions - Male, 32, brick layer. Female, 15, housekeeper. Male, 20, farm/field help. All listed among the dishes, silverware, draperies and furnishings to be sold with a house or other property. It hurt my heart so badly, to see that time after time, that after a while I gave up the research.

   We all know the old saying "there's always someone who has it worse than you". And it is true. I think, however, we've become so disconnected in our society - in our cubicles, our fenced yards - that though we *say* this, in reality we fail to actually be able to imagine a world beyond our "personal space". I am as guilty as anyone for this. Witnessing this week's events, however, made me *seriously* look beyond myself for the first time in a very long time. Sure, I've dispensed my fair share of advice to others, made a resolution to be kind(er..), turned my focus toward what I can to for others who find themselves walking this awful "grief journey". But none of that compared to even the most brief examination of myself in relation to the past of my own family, and the sacrifices they had to endure to not only make our current reality... well... *a reality*, but what had to happen for me *to even be*. Taking in and thoughtfully considering the fact that our Federal government had only struck down the anti-miscegenation laws (which called for interracial marriage to be illegal) in 1967, 5 short years before I was born to a married couple of different races - a black father and white mother.

   While you may think this is not at all related to my grief, my loss, think again. This is a post about *perspective*. My perspective changed greatly this week. And several times when I've wanted to feel down and overwhelmed these past few days, I've thought of my Grandmother's image from a very old family photo of her (along with several other generations of both of my

Life ain't always beautiful, but it's one hell of a ride...

grandparents families). I see her there, her three oldest children having already been born, surrounded by an old crooked wood porch and a bunch of dirt. Sitting there on that rickety porch, as poor as the dirt on which her chair was perched, she didn't dwell on her misfortune, rather, she and her husband dared to dream of a better life.

Maybe, just maybe, changing my perspective can change *my* life...

Take a moment to think about the blessings bestowed upon you by those who came before you, by those who have loved you and by those whom you've had the opportunity to call friend. Without whose incredible sacrifice your life may have ended up much different than it is, and not necessarily for the better.

27

WORDS LIKE VIOLENCE, BREAK THE SILENCE...
{ January 25, 2009 }

So the title of this post is culled from lyrics of a song that is really about the spoken word and how much the words we say can hurt one another, when in fact, we would rather judge ourselves and our relationships by our actions, rather than the things that we say (we'd all be best if we just shut up, basically). However, I feel that you don't have to have a conversation with anyone to feel the sting of words.

Today I did something that, while some of you may find ridiculous, was something that took me a couple of years to actually do. I changed my MySpace status to

Single.

MySpace, in its infinite wisdom and want to socially include everyone, oddly doesn't have a status for widows/widowers. Yes, ladies and gentlemen, they have a status for *SWINGERS*, but not widows. I guess they, too, think widows and widowers are old gals and geezers who spend their afternoons at the senior center, playing checkers and comparing snapshots of their grandchildren before heading out for a late supper (at 5PM) at

Applebee's. Not young, hip men and women who hang out on MySpace and keep their friends in the loop via Twitter.

A-holes.

Anywho, for most of this time since losing Ethan I had my status set as "in a relationship". I didn't want to seem as if I were in denial by continuing to list myself as "married" - I was aware that, technically, I was no longer married. However, I couldn't have felt further from single. I think it was honest to state that I was "in a relationship", because I really feel that I have still been in a relationship with Ethan, and until I reconciled the idea of no longer being in that relationship, that was the best way to describe myself.

Approaching two years since losing him, I feel that now is a good time for a status change for a couple of reasons.

First, and most notably, I am truly coming to a place where I no longer feel married to my husband. I miss him terribly, but I don't feel like his *wife* (I will post separately about my feeling about grieving the loss of Ethan vs. grieving the loss of my marriage). I am solo parenting, and making all of the decisions that we would have made as a couple, on my own. I am responsible for taking care of our family and home financially, on my own. Although I always consider what Ethan may have thought about this or that decision, that question, or subsequent answer, does not dictate how I function nor does it ultimately keep me from making a decision to do something that I know will benefit me personally, or our family overall. Of course this could be because I think, for the most part, that Ethan would have agreed with me on many of the decisions I've made, at least the major ones (probably a testament to our marriage, despite whatever issues we may have had during its course). As clichéd as this sounds, I truly DO believe that he would want me to do what is going to bring me and the girls happiness, I know

Life ain't always beautiful, but it's one hell of a ride...

this because he strived so very hard for that while he was alive, I can't imagine he'd want anything less in his death.

Secondly, and far less important, is the idea, especially at two years out, that I may be indicating that I am in a NEW relationship. As many people at my stage of the journey are either already dating or stepping back out into the world of dating, it's been indicated to me more than once that I was giving off some sort of signal that I am in a relationship with a new man. For the record I AM SO NOT, nor do I know if I am ready yet to wander down that road. At least, not for now.

"Not for now", you say?

Yes, not for now.

I don't know what my life has in store for me. But my relationship with Ethan taught me many things. One of those things is that I learned how wonderful it is to have someone with whom to share my life, my world, with. Someone who loves me completely for all of my positive attributes as well as all of my faults. Someone I'm not afraid to talk to about my life or my past with, someone who won't judge me for my mistakes. Someone who can accept with an open mind, and appreciate, where I've come from, and the person that I've worked very hard to become.

For so many years before meeting Ethan I thought I would be okay with being alone. As a matter of fact, I believed until I met him, that I *would* spend the rest of my life alone, that marriage was not "in the cards" for me. I stopped thinking about the life that I would one day have "when I got married", but rather, the life that I needed to begin building for myself and my daughter - and, having crossed over into my 30s, I was quite a bit behind the ball at that point. Now I find myself, (despite the best of intentions by the both of us) once again on my own, now with two children - a teen and a toddler - and once

Life ain't always beautiful, but it's one hell of a ride...

again thinking about the life that I better get to building for us. As much as I do not wish to close myself off to the potential that I may stumble into some sort of partner at some point in the future, I don't yet know if I am really ready for all of that at this point in my journey.

By changing my status to "single" I'm not indicating that I am "on the market", or "actively looking" or whatever, it just means I've come to terms with the idea that I am no longer Ethan's wife. Just another step along this road I travel, without a map, on my way to some unrecognizable destination...

28

HE GUIDED ME TO TENNESSEE
{ February 12, 2009 }

...and then dropped me off and said "later". I think I heard chuckling as he sauntered away...

I haven't posted in what feels like *ages*, but I've been so wrapped up in the move that I have hardly been able to think about anything else. I SWEAR if I ever do this again, I am selling everything and showing up to my new destination with my suitcase and a couple of kids.

If they're lucky (and I don't mean the suitcases).

Okay, that was a joke, I love my children. But if someone called CPS on me, it would just fit right in to an already ridiculous week and a half. Sigh...

Well, I really just popped in to clear out the cobwebs and chase away the crickets. Eventually I'll get my belongings (the ones that were guaranteed to arrive today but will be arriving - supposedly - on Sunday, though I won't be holding my breath) and can move from the hotel we're currently staying in to our new home. That might be nice.

A life in extended flux. It's not for the squeamish.

Life ain't always beautiful, but it's one hell of a ride...

29

THERE IS NO OTHER PILL TO TAKE.
SO SWALLOW THE ONE THAT MADE YOU ILL...
{ December 11, 2009 }

As of Tuesday, December 8, 2009, the person who is responsible for taking Ethan's life, greggory morris mcmillion, is a free man.

He served 26 months of a 6 year sentence. A 6 year sentence that was supposed to have a 60% minimum time requirement. So, essentially, he should not have been eligible for parole for another 2 years.

So, I'd like to give a big "thank you", a huge "shout out" if you will, to the California legislature, and its revered leader, Governor Schwarzenegger. To determine who gets a cot and who gets to walk, we prioritize certain crimes like, say, being an illegal immigrant and getting caught with a joint in your pocket. Instead of deporting them, we house them, at great expense to tax payers, in our prisons already bursting at the seams. Oh, and there's the handing down of long sentences to nonviolent, non-homicidal, drug based offenders, who sell their drugs to people who WANT to buy them. You know, willing parties to the activity. Instead, they choose to deal with overcrowding by turning loose convicts who are convicted of crimes like, you know, killing people who were **not** willing participants in their own deaths. Innocent victims....

mr. mcmillion is now home, comfortable and safe with his family in [....]. I'm sure in the very home he was trying to make his way back to that fateful night in February 2007 when he chose to make a u-turn on the freeway and proceed to rip Ethan away from this world and those of us who loved him dearly.

I'm sure mr. mcmillion's mother is THRILLED to have her son home for the holidays. Out of the "joint", all in one, safe, whole piece. What a phenomenal gift, to be sure! We, on the other hand, will never know the feeling. Going forward, we will only know the emptiness left on Christmas. Same as every Christmas for the past 2 years, same as the Christmas looming before us. Sure, things do get better. You can watch your 4 year old open presents without crying. You might even sing a Christmas song without nausea. But you can NEVER escape the emptiness....

If anyone is wondering (if you have to at this point in this post) - I have absolutely NO forgiveness for mr. mcmillion and I can say with confidence, I NEVER will. I have never stopped being angry with him. The mere mention of his name makes my hair stand on end. I wish I were a better person, but I can only be me.

But I DO have something to say to him:

Fuck you, greggory morris mcmillion. Fuck. You.

Life ain't always beautiful, but it's one hell of a ride...

30

ANOTHER BIRTHDAY...
{ December 12, 2009 }

Ethan

Today is the day that marks what would have been your 33rd birthday. For the third year I am left to celebrate what was your life, pondering all that was, that could have been, that will never be. I know these activities are futile, however, sometimes we can not anymore control the ways of the heart than we can the rising and setting of the sun. So here I am. Here we are...

This year Ava has many more questions than in previous years. She's gotten so big, and she is so unbelievably bright. I have unfortunately become the unwitting teacher of all kinds of lessons that little babies should not have to learn.

This year, as we did last, we went to the "party store" and picked out 12 balloons - 4 green "happy birthday", 5 plain white and 3 blue foil hearts - which we released from the back deck before sitting down to a scrumptious lunch of McDonald's chicken nuggets and "apple dippers". Ava was elected MC, so with a "Happy Birthday, Dada" and a quick NASA-esque countdown, she and I let go of our bunch-o-balloons and watched them sail off into the distance, toward what Ava believes is your "apartment in heaven".

Life ain't always beautiful, but it's one hell of a ride...

I just nod and say "yes" regarding such things. There is plenty of time for the cold, hard truth...

Anyway. Happy Birthday. Know that today, everyday, you are missed beyond words. That our love for you runs as deep today as it did the day you left us, and my memory of you is the most precious of all my possessions.

"We loved with a love that was more than love." ~ Edgar Allan Poe.

31

I'M DREAMING OF A WHITE CHRISTMAS
{ December 24, 2009 }

Well, I'm not exactly dreaming of one, I'm in the midst of one, quite frankly...

The weather outside is frightful....

We arrived yesterday to chilly temperatures and snow followed by freezing rain. Ava was so excited as our plane made it's approach into the airport in Madison, WI as she happily announced: "Look Mommy! Look at **all** the snow!"

Indeed, there was snow as far as the eye can see. I get so taken by the tree branches, which are so delicately, so perfectly swathed in ice, it looks painted on. 3 foot spear shaped, skull crushing icicles dangling from the eves... yeeeaaah... No, I'm not even kidding. Now, I've been assured they're harmless, but I give them a wide berth... just in case....

Spending the holidays with my in-laws is always fun and exciting, if not just a tad bittersweet. They are beautiful people, filled with love, warmth and humor (the apple didn't fall far from the tree), and they were so very excited to see their granddaughter. Ava having the opportunity to spend the Christmas holiday with them is a gift to us all, myself included. I am filled with happiness to know that Ava is surrounded by such love. They really know how to immerse themselves in the joys of the holiday, and I'm so glad that Ava will have these experiences, which will, no doubt, turn into wonderful memories for her.

On the other hand, revisiting my late husband's childhood home does bring about some sadness for me. When Ava and I visit, "our" room is the room that was Ethan's childhood bedroom. This is the same room that I've stayed in since the first time I was invited to the family home - first it was just Ethan and I, then the three of us: Ethan, Ava, and myself, with my older daughter getting her "very own" room next door. Now it's just Ava and me; I in the double bed, and Ava in her very own twin bed on the other side of the room. Last night before getting into bed, I sat for some time just taking in the energy of the room, looking over the few photos of him as a child that hang in the room, as well as our wedding portrait, which has been moved from the family room to this room. Now, I'm not entirely sure why it was moved in there, but I suspect one of two things: because I stay in that room, thus, perhaps it was assumed that I might like it in there, or it simply needed to go somewhere other than where it was because it was too painful for them to look at everyday. I think most likely, the latter gave way to the former. Honestly, now I don't mind so much that the picture is in there, but I will admit the first time I saw it in there, I was a little taken aback. I will also admit that I was a little sad that the picture had lost its place in the gathering spot of the home, to be moved to this seldom-used bedroom. Having said that, I do understand the reasoning (or at least my assumed reasoning), I guess I just... I don't know... wish it weren't so....

Anyway, on this, the eve of our third Christmas without Ethan, as I sit in the kitchen listening to Ava and grandpa playing piano in the living room (one of their very favorite activities to do together), as we **all** do our best to

Life ain't always beautiful, but it's one hell of a ride...

make this Christmas better than the last, I am reminded of how far we've come - how far I've come - in these three years. The hard, itchy scab of healing is finally beginning to reveal its gifts hidden beneath. The ability to embrace, no, ENJOY the beauty of the season and the love and acceptance extended to both my child and myself by his family is truly one of the greatest gifts of all.

32

BABY IT'S COLD OUTSIDE
{ December 25, 2009 }

Christmas in Wisconsin is always a, uh, *treat* weather-wise. After a "slow weather" day here yesterday, once again, Mother Nature has picked up where she left off two days ago, and it's been very steadily snowing since earlier this afternoon. Oddly enough, it started snowing just as I was preparing myself to go out and visit Ethan at the cemetery.

Why is that odd, you ask? Well....

Ethan's folks live in the Southern part of Wisconsin, which, unlike more northern towns like Green Bay, aren't always bombarded as badly with the harsh conditions the state, generally speaking, is so famous for. Which means there is slightly (if not much) less chance that there will be snow on Christmas. Of course, in the time I've been a member of this family, I've only witnessed such an occasion once: the year that our whole family came (Ethan, myself and both of the girls) for Ava's first Christmas at Grandma and Grandpa's.

Ethan couldn't WAIT to introduce Ava to snow. He was going to teach her how to build a snowman, how to sled, how to perfectly pack a great snowball. She would be his very apt pupil and eventually his very well trained snowball fight sidekick. Yes, at all of 16 months old.

Yet, when we arrived in his little hometown, much to his disappointment, there was nary a single flake of snow.

We watched.

We waited.

We noticed the temperatures rise and fall.

It rained.

Christmas came and went, and wasn't "white" at all. In spite of that, we enjoyed a wonderful day with the family, which included his 100 year old grandfather, who, sadly, left us about a year after Ethan.

As is tradition on his mother's side of the family, the day after Christmas we headed north for their annual "Festivus".

Yeah, you heard me. I said *Festivus.* Now, if you couldn't figure it out previously, you must now certainly know why I love these people....

This particular year brought the entire family, including Ethan's cousins who had moved to towns near and far, all with offspring in tow and all together in once place. Now that I think about it, perhaps our decision to make the trip that year was a bit of a hidden blessing in the fact that I do believe that was the last time that all of the cousins were together at Christmas. Every Christmas since there has been a cousin or two who couldn't make it for one reason or another, which I suppose is a common eventuality in large families. But I digress...

"Up North" there was tons of snow. In fact, so much snow that we almost didn't make it up there, having to turn back around at the halfway point of our first attempt due to the weather conditions. We headed out that next morning (round 2!) and made it there safely, though I was a nervous wreck all the way. It was a bit of a whirlwind, since we got there later than expected, so we really didn't get a chance to get out and play in the snow. The next day we were back at his parent's house, back to our "snow-less Christmas".

Less than two months later he would be gone.

Consequently, I made an unplanned, very unwanted trip to his little tiny hometown in the middle of February. It seemed that since we'd last visited winter had finally made her entrance, and she was really working hard making up for the lost time. We actually had to make our arrangements around whether or not we could manage to get flights, and family could travel safely, into town, the weather was so bad. On the day of his interment, it snowed an incredible amount of snow. It was freezing, it was gray. It snowed lots and lots of big fat "hey check me out, *I'm a big 'ole snowflake!*" snow. The scene, which I've played a million times over in my head, always comes across to me visually as rather Dickensian: the cemetery, with it's avenue of leaf-less trees covered in snow, somber and bitterly cold, blanketed in white. Ethan had wanted it to snow so badly for us that Christmas. Well, he got his snow. A little late, but he got it.

The Christmas following Ethan's death, I returned to this tiny town to spend the holidays with his parents with only Ava in tow.

There was white powdery snow into the horizon (of course!). Only now, it was I alone who took Ava out so she could make footprints in the snow and make a snowball. It was Grandpa who pulled her down the drive for her first ride on a sled. It was terribly sad. That Christmas was incredibly difficult for all of us, our first without him. I think it was good for us, his parents and I, to have one another and I'm very glad that we did. And I'm even gladder to be able to say that particular Christmas is far behind us...

Today was our second Christmas here at his parent's home since he's been gone. And today had a much better feeling than our Christmas of two

Life ain't always beautiful, but it's one hell of a ride...

years ago. This afternoon as I planned to pay a visit to him it began to snow. A nice, steady snowfall. I headed out on the all too familiar, though very short, journey to the cemetery on empty streets as everyone sat warm in their homes with their families. I turned into the cemetery and was overwhelmed by a feeling of familiarity. Not the normal feeling you get when you've been to the same place so many times, but the feeling of having experienced the same scene. It poured over me as I drove through the *avenue of leaf-less trees, covered in snow....*

I sat for some time beside him, all the while getting pelted in the face by freezing wet snow, which seemed to be coming much faster now. Like usual, I spent some time reflecting, however this time, for the first time, I didn't spend the duration talking to him and crying. Instead, I very quietly dug out a big heart in the snow. Made it nice and big and... empty.

But I know it won't stay that way. You see, by tomorrow, it will probably be almost completely filled with fresh snow. And that is a good thing. I've finally come to realize, after nearly 3 years, that empty hearts should not remain forever empty. They should be exposed to the world and the heavens to be filled. I guess that is the difference between this Christmas and Christmas 2007. Then I would never have believed that my empty heart could ever be filled - with *anything* - ever again. Now I truly believe that it is nature's way - to ensure that it is full eventually, should one have the faith and the courage to allow it to be exposed to the world and the heavens....

It's been snowing for hours now, in fact, it hasn't stopped since it started this afternoon. I can't help but think it has just a *little* something to do with Ethan. In just a little while I will officially have survived my 3rd Christmas since beginning this journey. How the time has flown. The house, for now, is quiet. I'm the only one still awake, listening to the clock ticking away (quite loudly, I might add), sipping what's left of my glass of Christmas wine. All things considered, I can honestly say today was truly a good day.

To my Ethan:

Merry Christmas. I hope that you are proud of the work I've done in these past few years in my effort to heal. No matter how I may go about filling my empty heart, know that you are with me all the while.

To all of you who walk this long, often solitary road:

Merry Christmas to you and yours, and may you find peace and comfort tonight.

Life ain't always beautiful, but it's one hell of a ride...

YEAR 4

{ or: that year I went from personal disaster to natural disaster }

They say time heals all wounds. And that statement, in its most basic context, I believe to be true – to a degree. What many people, especially those who may be in the throes of grief, may not realize (at least not right away) is that equally important to the passage of time, *is what you do with that time as it passes.* Why, or how, do some people manage to pull themselves relatively together in the course of a few years (or less), while some other people continue to drift through their lives, flailing their arms, trying not to drown in their raging sea of grief for years on end? Well, of course, there are many reasons for this, not least of which is the emotional and psychological health/stability/ability we come into our loss with, but one particular thing that I've observed time and time again is that those who seemed to find a sense of healing in a healthy manner within a few years are the ones who made healing their priority – taking an active role in rebuilding a life that has been torn apart, instead of passively waiting for it to rebuild itself.

Now, I realize that some of you who are reading this who have suffered the loss of your partner or spouse may be tempted to close this book, walk outside, and throw it in the burn pile. A few years ago that might have even been my own reaction, but before you do, just hear me out…

I've made no secret of my anger at having been thrust into this journey of widowhood. I was angry at the fact that a beautiful life was unfairly, and violently cut short in a way that was totally avoidable. I have been angry that our daughter will never know the amazing man her father was. I've been angry and saddened that lovely, kind people like my in-laws were dealt this tragedy. I have expressed my anger at the justice system, the young man who caused all of this in the first place, and even at my very innocent husband for leaving me here… *alone.* And it was okay to be angry. I think it is a totally natural and acceptable emotion for me to have felt given the circumstances.

But anger is a sword with two edges: with one it is possible to empower yourself toward change and justice, wielding it forth, slaying all that is wrong in your world (and the world beyond). With the other, however, if you are not careful you end up spending all of your time and energy just repeatedly injuring yourself.

I spent years injuring myself. And then wondering why I couldn't stop bleeding…

I tried many things in an attempt to escape my overwhelming *grief anger*, the feeling of absolute unfairness of it all that I simply couldn't seem to shake. I worked a billion hours a day, immersing myself in other people's careers and success. I shopped till I dropped – shoes and home accessories becoming my drugs of choice. As if I could somehow escape my pain by looking around my home and seeing lovely things, or if I had on expensive, beautiful shoes I would somehow forget how very broken I felt inside. I even moved 2,000 miles away to try to surround myself with new, untainted energy; to a place my husband never lived, where his ghost was not hiding in each and every corner. Certainly that ought to have done it.

Several hundred thousand dollars, and thousands of miles later, what I eventually learned (the most difficult and expensive way), is that you can not work away, buy your way out of, or run away from grief. Until you are willing to meet it face-to-face, it would always be there… waiting, no matter how much time had elapsed since your loss.

By the time I rolled into my 4th year, of course, plenty of *time* had gone by. And while I had far more moments of clarity than in the years preceding it, and I was able to embrace both the idea of change and the possibility of hope, I couldn't help but feel a bit… stifled. Like something was keeping me stuck in a place I no longer wanted to be, but couldn't seem to find the road out of.

* * * *

Once we had made the move to Nashville, I was fortunate enough to be able to spend a lot more time with both of my girls. I had the pleasure of being able to drop off and pick them up from school every day, an experience I looked at as a privilege – one I had never had previously because of my work commitments over the years. The morning and afternoon (trapped) in the car was a wonderful time to connect with my kids, especially my oldest daughter who was now in high school, and would only really have a conversation with me if I locked her in a fast moving steel box offering her little choice in the matter. It was one day as I was sitting in my car in the high school parking lot awaiting the afternoon dismissal, that I was struck with the most profound and seemingly out of the blue epiphany I had experienced since Ethan's death, perhaps the most important one that I had ever had at any point in my life. As I sat in my car in silence, a question popped into my head:

What have you learned?

Wait, what? What do you mean, what have I learned? I've learned that it sucks to be alone, and it's fucked up to have to bury your 30 year old husband. Also, I pretty much hate people, and I'm probably the worst parent… ever, and I hate that my kids are stuck with me and not E, because he definitely would have done all of this *way* better than I was doing.

No, Stephanie. Every event that happens to us in our lives contains something worth learning – some real wisdom. *What are the lessons that you've learned from 3 years of doing this*?

I was having a kind of *Karate Kid* moment. For 3 years I had been waxing and painting and all pissed off about the fact that I was waxing and painting. I wanted to feel better *damnit!* So why couldn't I move beyond waxing and painting? What was the point of all of this stupid wax and paint?

What I didn't realize was, I was too close to it to truly understand the big picture: hidden in the waxing and painting, were the ancient skills of a *life warrior.* I would be ready to move beyond waxing and painting when the techniques had become second nature. Of course, knowing technique is not good enough – you must apply everything you've learned in the practice ring, experience both success and failure so that you can learn and ultimately improve; the earned wisdom with each misstep and each win along the way making you a stronger, wiser, more effective warrior.

What I had learned was that the entire time I had wanted nothing but to sweep my grief and anger and sadness under a rug... or a pile of work, or a pile of (really nice) shoes. I wanted to hide in a far away place where it couldn't find me. And I wanted to call it "healing".

What I had learned was that none of that was actually helping me heal in any way – temporarily cope, perhaps yes, but *heal*? Nope.

What I had learned was that while time was now offering me a different perspective, it was also now telling me if I wanted to get over the top, I was going to have to *do the work.* To take direct action to help myself. To stop putting the burden on it (time), and take 100% responsibility for recreating, reshaping the pieces my own broken life.

What I had learned is that while I was sweeping my own loss under the rug, I was inadvertently sweeping my children's loss under the rug as well. And I was not setting a good example for either of them regarding how to cope when life throws some awful, terrible stuff your way. And I learned that I really wanted to be a positive example to them, not only as their mother, but as a *woman* trying to get along in this world – which can be full of awful, terrible stuff. I wanted them to grow up to be strong, healthy women, and that began with me.

   I also learned that when we encounter enlightenment, we have an obligation to share it with as many people as we possibly can.

   I had left my career in music and entertainment behind to venture out in search of my own sense of healing and peace, but also to discover a life path that I felt was more *purposeful.* That day, sitting in my daughter's high school parking lot, I believed that I had discovered that purpose: to actively search for the wisdom in my grief and healing journey, to put that wisdom into practice in every possible area of my own life, and to help other people who find themselves facing the loss of their loves to do the same for themselves.

   During the 4th year of my journey I would launch a website for other young widows and widowers called R.I.S.E. (an acronym for release, inspiration, strength, evolution). I still had tons to learn, but I was finally open to the idea of being an *active* learner – with my ears and eyes wide open, instead of passively hiding and hoping that this healing thing would just take care of itself.

   This new perspective would prove to be well timed. One year after I moved to Nashville, my adopted town would experience one of the most devastating floods in the city's history, followed by my mother's cancer diagnoses. Before my parking lot epiphany I would never have been capable of viewing such a devastating events as indicators that I was actually in the right place at the right time, because there were valuable lessons to be learned from it, or that my learned wisdom would help me cope and enable me to help my mom through the greatest challenge of her life.

   When we are standing right up to something (an event, or a life challenge), we can only see what is right in front of our eyes. Stepping back a

Life ain't always beautiful, but it's one hell of a ride...

few paces, away from a thing, helps us take it in with much wider perspective – you can see what's going on in the frame to the left and to the right, above, below, and all around. Time then, is like taking a few paces back allowing us to see "the bigger picture". The picture, of course, is the same as it ever was, you just have a better place from which to interpret the meaning behind the imagery, now that instead of only being able to see one tiny piece up close (you and your pain), you can actually see more of it (the rest of your life).

33

I WANNA TALK ABOUT MII
{ January 31, 2010 }

My 4 year old LOVES her Wii, most particularly the game Wii Sport Resort. Most of you are probably familiar with the system, but for those who aren't, with the Wii you have the ability to create your own characters that you then use to play your games. Building your own characters allows you to save points/scores, etc.. The characters you create are appropriately (and cleverly) referred to as a "Mii"....

Today we were sitting around the house (it *is* Sunday) and Ava was playing Wii in the other room. She came into the kitchen, where I was, and asked a question about her dad, which I answered, then she ran out of the room. A minute or two later, she ran back in, asked another question, and with another satisfactory answer, ran out again. She came back a third time, asked yet another question, and it was then that it occurred to me that all of the questions were esthetic questions regarding her fathers looks/features.

Now, she was only 18 months when her dad was killed, so while she knows him in photos and has a general idea of his image, it's understandable that she would be a little fuzzy on some of the details ("Mom, what color are my dad's eyes?"). I decided to follow her back into the family room where I discovered why she had been asking all of the questions: she was making a "Mii". So I sat down with her and helped her: it has a place for the Mii's favorite

Life ain't always beautiful, but it's one hell of a ride...

color, so I let her know that his was green, helped her pick out just the right goatee, etc.

The name for this Mii?

DAD

I have noticed recently that she has had a lot more questions and thoughts about her dad, and "Dada is in heaven" is no longer sufficient. She is a very bright child (reading since 2), so I always knew she would be ready with questions long before I would be ready to give her answers.

I think I'm entering into a new phase with her, and I guess I'm a little apprehensive. I've had the luxury - and I know that it absolutely is a luxury - of being able to postpone having to deal with my child's loss of her father, which I realize has been of great benefit to me as I've been able to focus on myself, on my own healing, which I know many people do not have the liberty of doing.

I'm fearful, I guess, because I feel that I'm opening up a big 'ole can of worms that I'm really not sure I know how to deal with. Or maybe I am just afraid of having to answer things that I don't have the answer to, and I know once I open the door, there will be a continuous flow of traffic - in the form of questions and observations - that I will have to deal with somehow.

Or, I am just not so eager for my little angel to have to face the reality of what is, because what is *is painful*, and it's our job to protect our children from all of the bad stuff.... Right?

34

TELL IT LIKE IT IS
VALENTINE'S DAY EDITION
{ February 14, 2010 }

Valentines Day Singles: Everything you seek, you already possess.

The greatest love of all is found within.

...This is TRUTH not consolation.

35

DO YOU KNOW WHAT TODAY IS...
{ February 19, 2010 }

....It's our anniversary.

Today is what would have been our 5 year wedding anniversary. My third year without him, I've now been widowed longer than I was actually married....

What will I do with myself today? Well, mostly reflect - on our relationship, on the gift of love (and it is a gift), on what I've learned since he's been gone, on my path forward. This is actually my *fourth* anniversary without him, technically, he was killed one day before our 2nd wedding anniversary (so I got through that "first", well, immediately), and while that seems so strange when I really think about it, I am glad to be able to say at this point the approach to the date did not bring the sheer dread that preceded my anniversary in previous years, nor did I wake up this morning awash in a sea of despair.

No, to the contrary, I can honestly say that I'm able to once again view this as a *good day*.

As it should be. Today marks the day I was joined as one with a wonderful man with a beautiful spirit. A man who brought to me the gift of unconditional love and unquestionable friendship, and taught me not only the joys of family, but, in no uncertain terms, I learned the hardest way the value of time. Everything that I've received from having known him, having loved him, and yes, even having lost him, is absolutely positive. Of course, saying that is not in anyway meant to discount the overwhelming grief that took, in my case, years to work through, but having managed my way through it (and by "it", I simply mean the grief), I was able to realize that there were valuable lessons to be learned and actions to be taken, I learned that it was not only okay, it was essential, to *change lanes* - to have the clarity and courage put my life on it's correct path...

What happened to my husband was an inexplicable tragedy that could, and SHOULD, have been avoided. There is not a day that goes by that I don't think of Ethan. I've cried at least 10 million tears and yet, he hasn't returned. I've not woken to find that it was all just a trip into some different dimension and that he's been here, waiting for me, the entire time. The bottom line is: I can not change what happened, and I am still here with children to raise, bills to pay and a life to live, or NOT live. The latter - the life to live -being the only aspect, really, that is totally within my control. Well, I not only choose to live, I choose to live with joy and love and positivity and hope.

Making that decision was one of the most liberating acts I've ever committed.

Make no mistake, he is still here with me. Living in positivity in no way means that I've "gotten over" or "left behind" my husband in any way. In fact, in a way it's probably the closest I can get to an appropriate tribute to the person that he was...

So, today, I will smile at the positive memories of *our* past, while at the same I will look forward with a positive, open mind, toward *my* future.

Life ain't always beautiful, but it's one hell of a ride...

...And I might just go out and do something nice for myself. After all, it IS my anniversary ;-)

36

TELL IT LIKE IT IS
{ March 9, 2010 }

An angry heart can **not** heal. You must first let go of the negativity in order to make room for positivity and love. You can not undo what has been done, so do yourself a favor and release it....

37

TELL IT LIKE IT IS
{ March 11, 2010 }

Waiting for your heart to heal? Don't. Time does not "heal all wounds", least of all a broken heart. While healing certainly takes a period of time, it also (mostly) takes WORK.   So be active in your healing, you'll be amazed at not only the healing transformation going on in your heart, but perhaps you'll find that the transformation begins to affect many other aspects of your life in positive ways!

38

TO EVERYTHING TURN, TURN, TURN
{ March 15, 2010 }

Ahhh, Spring. As the temperatures get warmer, the grass, once again, begins to grow and daffodils and tulips poke their colorful heads out as the early harbingers of the wonderful changes to come.

And as Mother Nature takes care of things outside, we tend to wake up to the yearning to start, once again, taking care of things inside. As we shake off the cobwebs of winter, and all the heavy layers of clothing, we begin to embrace the promises of a new spring. Our homes get a "spring cleaning", and many of us find a renewed desire to get back on track with plans we often put aside when it becomes too cold (and laborious) to venture outside, and the ever present gray skies temper the flames of our desires

Personally, the onset of this particular Spring seems to have awakened my long dormant brain cells into action, I'm suddenly feeling "fired up" to take on all sorts of projects. Some things I've been meaning to do for ages, some new things I've just added to my list. Some personal matters long overdue attention, and many more issues pertaining to my career (or, lack thereof, as it were).

I've always been a great list maker, an organizer, a planner. Before losing E, I can honestly say, I was great at the execution as well. Something happened the day he died, though. It's like my drive to follow through with *anything* was buried right along with him.

Now, I know this is not unusual. We need our energy for healing, and taking care of the necessities, the basics. We widows are hard-pressed to accomplish anything more than that (even the basics are nearly impossible some days). I've spent a lot of time focusing my energy on healing, and I believe that I've come a LONG way in the past few years. So far in fact, that I finally possess the wherewithal to look around myself and honestly say (out loud), "It's time to get back on track".

And so with that, I've begun - making lists, researching, being honest with myself about who I am now and what it is I truly want to accomplish. Asking myself how I want to raise my children, what kind of example I want to be to my girls. What kind of example do I want to be to others that are on this same journey, or who will, no doubt, walk this road after me?

And I've come to some conclusions...

"Back on track" doesn't necessarily mean the *same* track I was on 3 years ago. I am definitely not the girl I used to be, so why would my *track* be? Quite contrary: I'm better - stronger, wiser, and if I could pull myself away from this desk and the internet I'd probably be faster, too. My focus today is vastly different than it was 3 1/2 years ago when my husband was still here, and my healing work has brought a sense of positive understanding about myself that I can not say with confidence I would have ever achieved had I not been forced down this, horrible, almost unbearable path. Which brings me to this "lesson" nonsense I've been going on about lately. I have searched long and hard and I believe that it's finally become evident to me what the lesson in all of this is, and as each day passes, it seems to just keep unfolding. As it does, so does my fascination and my growing need regain my drive to "make it happen", a seemingly long lost skill of mine honed during those music business years and all but obliterated during my grieving years...

Well, I'm dusting it off, and putting it back into action. Only in a kinder, more gentle way. Part of the lesson, as it has become clear to me, is that I am in control of my own destiny. So I'm best to grab a hold of it and start shaping it into what I wish for it to be.

Life ain't always beautiful, but it's one hell of a ride...

39

TELL IT LIKE IT IS (DRAFT POST)
{ never published }

Intelligence is often mistaken to be synonymous with wisdom, but they are not necessarily one in the same. While they can certainly mix (and mix well!) you can absolutely posses one without the other. Be cautioned against clinging to the words of a man simply because he is well read, likewise, be careful not to dismiss a man simply because he is not....

40

BE A HAPPY MAN.
I TRY THE BEST I CAN
{ March 28, 2010 }

...Or maybe I'm just looking for too much...

Anyone who knows me, knows that as much as I may long to be "outgoing" I am just not a social butterfly. I will never win the title of "Miss Congeniality" no matter how much I dress up and show up, the smile always seems just a bit contrived. This is due to a little known fact about me, a fact that often leads to a lot of misunderstanding about me: It's not because I'm not happy to be there. It's because I'm *terrified* to be there...

I guess what I have, would really be "borderline" in terms of social anxiety, although there have been occasions where I've had to literally go home because the anxiety became too overwhelming. This anxiety has kept me back personally - noted by my lack of friends - and it's kept me back professionally - as demonstrated by the fact that although I had the most fortunate opportunity to work with some of the biggest names in music, I would always sit myself in a corner while everyone else interacted, believing, for whatever reason, that I wasn't worthy of sharing the same space unless it was to perform some very specific task. Speak only when spoken to, as it were. You're not important... Just stay out of the way...

Life ain't always beautiful, but it's one hell of a ride...

Ethan was definitely the more personable member of our partnership. He was the one that people liked. He was the goof ball, and I believe, the more intelligent one, though, perhaps, I might have been considered more "wise" having had much more life experience. But that lack of life experience coupled with his jovial nature might be the very thing that allowed him to be so positive, so happy. He was a friend magnet...

We were raised very differently and had *very* different childhood experiences. His parents nurtured his talents and openly supported his goals, they were educators who gave their kids lots of educational opportunities. My parents, well, were... different... than that. Let's just say I learned most of my lessons from the school of hard knocks. This contrast was obvious, I think, in the difference in our levels of self-esteem. Sure, Ethan was always nervous about meeting with new clients, concerned about whether or not a client was going to like his work, etc., however, as a person, I don't think he walked around with the idea that he wasn't worthy of friendship or love, that he wasn't likable as a person. He's always had those things in his life - friends, love, acceptance - so he had no reason to doubt whether or not he was deserving. In fact, I know he was aware that his personality opened up, and/or kept open, a lot of doors that probably would have been closed to me, had I been in his position. He knew how to shake what his mama gave him: a big fat smile and a friendly, truly caring personality, and it won him legions of fans in the form of friends.

Last night I had the occasion to attend a fundraiser for my youngest child's school. Now, she attends a very nice private school here in Nashville, one that has a stellar reputation and whose student body is made up of children of some very well educated, successful, and in many instances, well known members of the community. Most importantly, they seem to really be catering to my daughter's advanced abilities in many areas and fostering her curiosity and diverse interests academically and creatively, and for that, they get my seal of approval. And while my little one loves her school and friends and is growing in all kinds of wonderful ways, *I've* had a very hard time handling the adjustments required as a solo parent of a child attending a private school.

Solo parent. Not to be confused with *single* parent. In my, um, *situation*, there is no other parent to attend functions with - you know, that "get-along-for-the-sake-of-the-kids" thing where both parents show up, with or without new partners, because everyone is focused on the best interest of the child. Granted, those situations are often not ideal. "Grinning and bearing it" can be a very hard task, indeed, and I do not dismiss that fact.

To be clear, I've not had any kind of adverse treatment or negativity from any of the teachers or parents at the school. It's that I just don't really feel that I "fit in" there (for a myriad of reasons). Of course, where my child attends school is determined by what is best for my child, not by what is best for me. However, having said that, when your child attends private school, there is an elevated expectation that parents be "fully engaged" in their child's education, participating in school events, showing up to functions, volunteering when the need arises. And there are lots of events, functions and *arising needs*...

Last night, as I sat in a corner by myself, working a coke down to the last ice cube, I thought (a lot) about how different this experience would be if Ethan were here. I don't do that much these days, I've worked very hard on my healing, and I've had 3 years of "situations", of "life stuff" that I've worked through. The school thing, though, is a brand new thing. Our youngest child was only a baby when Ethan passed away, so it's not like we had a child in

Life ain't always beautiful, but it's one hell of a ride...

school and we were known as a couple and we did all this stuff together and now I have to attempt to do it all on my own. We never had a chance to do this stuff together. So I am really just assuming it would be different if he were here... right?

I can safely assume that, at the very least, I wouldn't have to attend these things alone - most of the time anyway. I know darn well that because he worked the most God-awful hours there is no real guarantee that he would, in fact, be available to attend every function or event, but I can easily and pretty accurately assume that he would be able to on occasion. I can also safely assume that when he could go, he'd naturally do better at connecting with the other parents. Yeah, that whole "makin' friends" thing. Something that I've not learned how to do, even after 38 years on this old rock. That leads to the assumption that since he'd have gone out like a warrior and rounded up friends, when I did have to attend these things on my own, I wouldn't have to sit alone in a corner - my wonderful, dutiful husband having endeared several of the other parents to us (read: him), there would be lots of

- Oh, where's Ethan tonight?

- Oh, you're on your own?

- Have a seat with us!

Instead there's just me.

Me with my lack of ability to endear myself to anyone.

Last night there were no oh, you're on your owns, no have a seat with us's...

And it's my own fault. I know this. My friends are my responsibility, as is my own happiness. But, I know my person. I know my limitations. While I feel the *solitude* of being solo while alone at my home, I'm not slapped with that deep feeling of *loneliness* that I get when I attempt these types of functions. Perhaps I should simply stop putting myself in to this negative position. But, I know that without putting myself out there, there is absolutely no chance that this will EVER change. One of the things I've gained in these past few years, through all of *this*, is the very idea hope. So maybe I should keep showing up in the hope that this situation, my situation, will change itself. Like the sun finally exposing itself after years behind a horribly large black cloud (cue the chorus of angels: "aaaaahhhhh!!!") and just like *THAT*, I will suddenly become a smiling, confident, hand shaking - no, no... HUGGING (nothing freaks me out more than a stranger coming toward me with open arms) - HAPPY woman that people will want to know.

    ...Or, maybe I'm just looking for too much....

41

BLINDLY I IMAGINED
I COULD KEEP YOU UNDER GLASS
{ April 5, 2010 }

I am the parent of a 15 year old. Parenting a teen can be challenging under the best of circumstances, however, I have come to realize, and I'm now prepared to admit, that my experience with traumatic loss is severely affecting my decision making as a parent. I am also prepared to admit that it is not in complete fairness to my daughter, and I really need to do something about it. For her sake... and mine....

It seems I am in the midst of raising one very, ahem, *spirited* young lady. On occasion she feels it very necessary to give me a piece of her mind. While I neither appreciate, nor condone the (cough) forthrightness of her execution, a couple of nights ago she said something that was not altogether wrong. She was raving on about how she is not allowed to do *anything*, that everything has to be *my way or no way* at all.

Okay, I'm the parent, so what's wrong (or unique) about this situation, you ask? I'm sure that this very same conversation has been repeated at least a billion times in a billion different households. Perfectly normal parents and teens at odds about the boundaries set by well meaning, loving parents. It's not as if her friends are allowed to just run amok and do whatever they wish, whenever they wish, they have boundaries and rules, too. But, beyond being a normal parent with a normal teen, there is additional fear that drives my decision making when it comes to her:

Having been stung by the trauma of incredibly traumatic, sudden loss, I am determined to do whatever is possibly within my control to avoid a repeat of the experience.

...Going out in the evening with other parents dropping off/picking up? Oooooh. Ummmm. Yeah, but call me... repeatedly...

...Staying over night at *that* girl's house? That girl with the boyfriend who has a car? Hmmm. You can go visit if her parents come pick you up, but you can't stay the night (yeah, I know that game)...

...Riding with other teens? Nope. Not even during the day. Don't bother asking...

...Learning how to drive? A *car*?? Oh, forget about it (it doesn't matter that I learned at 14 and she's now 15 1/2)...

Of course, it was being in a car that led to the end of Ethan's life, so I guess many would understand my auto-phobia (is that a thing? Anyway, you get it). I am terrified of my own children being in the car with me - not because of my driving skills (which, of course, are absolutely perfect), but because I can not control the actions of all of the other drivers. Complacent drivers. Texting drivers. Inexperienced, unknowledgeable drivers. Selfish, thoughtless drivers. Distracted drivers. *Drunk* drivers...

But then there is everything else: if she goes out, she can get separated from her friends and, ending up alone, could become easy prey to an abductor (did you know that 2100 kids are reported missing per DAY in America? Granted, a large majority are family abductions or runaways, but, still, many are not...). With her under-developed judgment skills, she could meet someone she *thinks* is nice and end up in terrible danger. She can be sitting in the food court (or the classroom, or wherever) and someone could walk in and shoot up the place, and her bulletproof super mom wouldn't be there to protect her...

I can not seem to wrap my brain around the idea that she can go out with her friends, try on a few clothes, grab some fries and a coke in the food court, giggle about boys and come home to me as safe and sound, as whole, as she left me, something done by millions of teens every day in America. Something done by me and my friends when we were her age. However, it's hard for me to look at the world as the same place it was back then. Partly because I'm no longer a teen, I'm a parent; so my perspective is a bit broader of course, but also because, well, it just *isn't...* is it?

My experience has taught me that I am not untouchable. We, our family, are not immune to unbearable, life changing tragedy. Bad - horribly bad - things happen to perfectly good people just going about their daily lives. This is not the stuff of movies or OTHER people on tv The reality of just how quickly a human life can be snuffed out and the myriad of unbelievably avoidable ways in which people's lives are ended every day is mind boggling. Trust me, my mind has been boggled to the nth degree. Having scraped and scratched my way from "boggled" to "slightly bewildered", I have no desire to ever go back to that place...

Most of all, though, I want my daughter to have a chance to grow into the beautiful, bright woman I know she is destined to be. To have the chance to experience a full, wonderful, LONG life. And I know that starts now. I know that her life will be a combination of all of its parts, and her experiences now will shape who she is in the future. I worry that by not allowing her to spread

Life ain't always beautiful, but it's one hell of a ride...

her wings and enjoy a certain amount of freedom, I am not only depriving her of a full, happy, and memorable childhood, I am possibly inhibiting, or at least delaying, the development of necessary life skills that should be honed for many years before our children are let out from underneath *our* wings to spread theirs and navigate the world on their own. After all, our greatest lessons come from our own life's experiences.

Yes, our greatest lessons come from our own life's experiences.

Which leads me back to square one. I have learned this behavior from my own life's combined experiences, of which losing Ethan was the proverbial icing on the slightly burnt, lopsided cake. All the regret and the shame and the hurt and the trauma and the loss and the sorrow and the grief - and now those experiences are stifling my ability to release my child so that she has ability to have *her own* life experiences. In her moments of overflowing frustration she will often point this fact out to me, which, of course, only serves to fan the flames of my fear - instead of "Mom, I understand that there are real dangers out there, and I am always very aware of my environment and try to make good decisions about my safety", I get "GAWD MOM! You always think something BAD is going to happen. NOTHING is going to happen!" (huff. stamp. stomp... stomp... stomp... SLAM).

But something could happen... Right.......?

I know what you're thinking, but this is not an entirely selfish thing. I would think that the majority of parents strive in their own ways to attempt to protect their children from all harm - physical and emotional. However, I will admit that having spent time reassembling the pieces of a broken heart, time that was not counted in months, but rather, in *years*, and attempting to (currently) nurse back to health what can best be described as a fractured life, as principal motivators. Worrying about my daughter out there, alone, in the "great wide open" is honestly more than I think I can bear at this point in my life.

And I know that is not fair to her...

I know that this is something that I need to try to reconcile sooner rather than later. I need to figure out how to overcome my fears, borne from my knowledge and experience in this world, so that I do not end up imparting my fears on her, or worse, so that she doesn't begin to believe that her freedom will only be found by running as far from me as possible. I need to somehow overcome my apprehension of, well, *the world*, so that I can lift the cloche and stop stifling her need - her right - to see and do and grow and experience... to live... to fly...

42

NEVER KNOWING WHAT COULD HAVE BEEN
{ April 20, 2010 }

It doesn't seem to matter how far from our loss we roam, every once in a while it seems to catch up with us in some way or another.

I believe that I reached a healing place regarding losing Ethan some time ago. Since that time I've turned my focus to assisting others on their road to healing in various ways. I'm excited about this new focus, it is something that I find a great deal of joy in doing - I am really striving to be someone that people feel that they can turn to for help, and I truly hope that as time goes on, that I am able to touch people in a positive way. However, sometimes it feels that by making the decision to reach out to help others that I have some sort of requirement to be "happy" or "positive" at *ALL* times, otherwise it might send the message that my heart really hasn't healed at all, and if I haven't been able to achieve healing myself, how could I ever be of any assistance to anyone else?

Truth is, my heart is quite well. Having said that, I do get struck with certain negative emotions from time to time when I allow my mind to wander - fruitlessly, pointlessly - down paths with signs that read things like "What If" road, "You Should Have" lane, "Things Would Be SO Much Different Now" avenue, and the like. I haven't noticed any particular triggers for it, and I find, these days, that it doesn't happen all that often. But when it does, it still manages to really knock me for a loop, though I'm never down as long as I would have been, say, a couple of years ago.

Anyone who has journeyed down the road of widowhood probably understands this feeling I'm talking about. You sit, usually alone, thinking how much better your life would be right now if you'd never lost your spouse. All the things you would be able to do or that you would be doing. Perhaps how much better your family life would be, the things you might have that you perhaps can no longer afford as a single income earner. And then, of course, there's that whole idea that you wouldn't be so darn lonely.

The bad times would be better, the good times, well, they'd be GREAT!

In actual fact, while I would give anything to have Ethan back, I can't truly say "what else" might be going on in our lives at this point. How happy we would really be at this point, 3 years later. Our kids wouldn't be perfect, and our marriage would very likely have its issues, as it did before he died. Would we still have the beautiful home I sold (at a horrific financial loss) last year? I ended up losing my job, and as our industry continues to shrink, who's to say he would have continued to make enough money to take care of all 4 of us? Would THAT have caused additional stress on our marriage? Would we have imploded? Would we have divorced? Of course, I like to think not. I like to think we had a strong enough love for one another that we would have weathered whatever storm - together - that came our way. My point, however, is that when my mind starts to wonder about all of those wonderful things I'm missing, it never, oddly enough, wanders to any of the *negative* things that may have had a similar chance of happening had he never passed away. Of course, he'd be alive, which would be fantastic ANY way you sliced it - I'd have my husband, my children would have their father, my in-laws would have their beloved son. But the rest? *Who really knows....*

　　　And honestly, good "what if's" or "bad what if's", what IS the point in wasting time pondering the "what if's" at all? He is gone and he is not coming back. I know this quite clearly, and I've come to terms with it in my heart. I guess every once in a while I need to remind my HEAD that I am best to leave aside the useless speculating and keep on shufflin' on in a forward direction. Best to focus my energy, that precious resource, on more positive endeavors right now, than unanswerable, unattainable hypotheticals borne of a past that is long behind me. I will embrace today and do the best I can with it, because no matter how I got here and whether I like it or not, THIS is where I am.

"When you realize how perfect everything is,

you will tilt your head back and laugh at the sky"

~ Buddha

43

ANGELS WITH SILVER WINGS, SHOULDN'T KNOW SUFFERING
{ April 25, 2010 }

There are times when, as a sole parent, I feel as if I'm carrying the weight of the world on my shoulders. When I say "sole" parent, I mean only parent. There is no other parent around to pick up the kids every other weekend. There is no one that can in-case-of-emergency run and grab the kids from school and make sure they are fed while I wrap up whatever it is I happen to be caught up in. There is no one sending me a check every month to cover our joint childcare expenses. There is no one with whom I can converse to come to a joint decision regarding any aspect of our children's lives. There is no one else who is obligated to spend time with these kids so mommy can get a break...

There's just me.

Just me trying to figure out how to take care of two kids - physically, financially, emotionally. Just me trying to make all of the right decisions regarding their lives and futures, their education, their social activities. Just me paying the bills, buying the food, clothing them and trying to keep up with "all of the things kids these days need".

And I'm often very exhausted by it.

Life ain't always beautiful, but it's one hell of a ride...

And I often think "I didn't sign up for this".

And sometimes I get angry.

And sometimes my kids get the short end of the stick because Mommy is sad about having been left here to do this alone. Because Mommy is annoyed, for lack of a better term, at having to do everything completely by herself. Mommy is frustrated by the fact that she is the only cook, cleaner, chauffeur, laundress, bath-giver, lunch-fixer, problem solver, story-listener, lap and cuddle-provider, cash-dispenser, nurse, worrier, warrior, protector, nose-wiper, butt-wiper, hair-doer, driving instructor, dictator, last minute project completer, tech support, emotional support and life guide....

And I usually end up feeling bad for my action/reaction/inaction. However, I shortly thereafter excuse myself because, after all, my husband's dead. And I didn't ask for this. And it isn't fair. And I should be given a little bit of slack... Right?

This morning, as I stood locked in the bathroom alone (the only place of privacy from my 4 year old shadow) staring at myself in the mirror, my thought suddenly shifted from my own reflection to the little person I could feel standing right outside the door, from whom I was hiding and who was nonetheless anxiously awaiting an invitation to join me. And it occurred to me, as clear as day:

My kids didn't ask for this either.

How unfair I have been to them to have thought "I" instead of "we"! How unfair I have been to consider my loss, my pain, above theirs! How unfair I have been to compound all that they didn't ask for, with more stuff they didn't ask for, negative experiences they certainly did not and do not deserve. I, of all people, should know better! They are beautiful, emotional, trusting little people who have asked for nothing but protection,

Life ain't always beautiful, but it's one hell of a ride...

guidance and love. The universe will undoubtedly hand them plenty more of that which they never ask for. It is my duty as their mother - as their sole parent - to protect them from such things, and to provide them with only those things that they do deserve, and none of the things that they do not.

I am a firm believer in fresh starts, and there is no better time, in my estimation, than right now for me to start viewing my role as parent with this fresh perspective. With all of the hurt they have suffered, I must ensure that they are not forced to suffer mine...

"Parents exist to teach the child,

but also they must learn what the child has to teach them;

and the child has a very great deal to teach them."

~ Arnold Bennett

44

THESE ARE DAYS YOU'LL REMEMBER
{ April 28, 2010 }

Today marks the 1,166th day since my husband's death. They are certainly days I remember. Well, with the exception of those early days when I was in what I can only describe as a walking coma.

- I remember days where I cried so much I was sure I would need a saline drip to re-hydrate, I thought there couldn't possibly be a drop of moisture left in my entire body.
- I remember the day I first saw the face of the man who took Ethan's life.
- I remember the day I laughed again for the first time. Really laughed - out loud - and didn't feel guilty.
- I remember the day I went back to his grave for the first time, nearly a year after I left him there. I remember the guilt I felt for leaving him alone for so long.
- I remember the day, just over a year after losing Ethan, someone at a "grief organization" (no less) told me that I was too far along in my grief (too far out from my loss) to get the help that I sought. It was the first time, but not the last, I'd feel the sting of society's misunderstanding of grief.

Life ain't always beautiful, but it's one hell of a ride...

- I remember the day I realized I wasn't the first person, nor the last, on earth to experience losing their husband at 35. And I remember feeling at once oddly comforted and terribly sad.
- I remember the day I had to celebrate our daughter's birthday without him for the first time.
- I remember the day I realized that I was marking what would be the first of many, many of his birthdays he would not be here to celebrate.
- I remember the day I realized that I had people in my life that really cared about me.
- I remember the day I understood that some of those people were having as much difficulty as I was dealing with their grief.
- I remember the day I discovered that no one could decide what was right for me in my grief aside from me.
- I remember the day it hit me: there was a lesson - and subsequently went on an active search to figure out, and fully understand what that lesson was.
- I remember the day I understood fully, and accepted that his dying was not my fault.
- I remember the day our youngest child asked where her dada lived (and I remember fumbling through a completely inadequate reply).
- I remember the day I was told that the person who took Ethan's life was to be freed. Free to walk and love and live. And I remembered to forget all of the hard work I'd done in my healing and found myself in a very dark place.
- I remember the day I came to understand that nothing, and no one, could heal me but me.
- I remember the day that I decided I wanted to live.

Life ain't always beautiful, but it's one hell of a ride...

- I remember clearly the day, the moment, when I realized it was time to let go of the 10,000 lbs. of hurt, it served me no purpose but to weigh me down, like a cinder block dragging me to the deepest depths of the sea...

I will *always* remember these days. Many of them hurt terribly, but that is not what they will be remembered most for. Rather, they are the days that continually force me to seek, to learn, to grow, to stand strong, to listen, to give, to let go. These are the days that have forced open my eyes till they burned, to make sure I didn't blink through a single nanosecond. And my eyes and my arms are as open as they've ever been, ready to see and embrace all the days ahead...

Life ain't always beautiful, but it's one hell of a ride...

45

NO ONE BELIEVED
THE WATER WOULD COME
{ May 7, 2010 }

No one could have predicted what happened here in Nashville this weekend. Unrelenting rains over a 48 hour period finally stopped, but Mother Nature was not finished. As the waters ran off from hills and ditches into creeks and from creeks into rivers, the peaceful, lazy rivers that wind through this wonderful city began to rise. And they rose, and they rose until they rose beyond their banks and overtook cars, homes, and highways. For several days we stayed glued to our televisions watching ground and aerial coverage of boat rescues and trying to wrap our collective minds around what, exactly, was going on.

Our 100 year flood plain was in the midst of a 500 year flood.

When the sun finally appeared and the temperatures rose, we began to hear the stories: stories of loss, stories of fear. We heard from families who'd lost loved ones and families who have loved ones who were still unaccounted for. But what we saw mostly were people who had finally been granted permission to return to their homes, only to find that everything they owned had been destroyed by those very swollen rivers. It was in listening to these people tell their stories - of total loss of all of their possessions, and

Life ain't always beautiful, but it's one hell of a ride...

destruction of homes and businesses - that I was struck by one very common and unexpected theme.

Gratitude.

One after another the various news channels would interview people as they tore walls to the studs, as they piled all their waterlogged, now worthless belongings, a lifetime's worth of items, and one after another they would each say the same thing: although they were sad about the items or homes they had lost, they were grateful, for *they were still here*. And, ultimately, they would get through this and things would be good again.

I am amazed at this... phenomenon. And very inspired by it.

I have discussed (ad nauseam) my belief that in every life event there are lessons. In the beginning, to be honest, when the rivers began their rapid ascent my first thought was that I had just moved here to get away from negativity and the distress I felt following Ethan's death, and now, barely a year later, I found myself surrounded by disaster - literally! But as I continued to watch, to listen, I began to realize that there were several positive lessons in what was happening to my newly adopted city. The two most prevalent are those regarding the value and spirit of community and, most importantly, gratitude.

I am grateful that my family and I are safe and well, and our homes are dry. I am grateful for the ability to be here to witness this community come together and take care of one another, and already, 5 days from the worst flooding, already working together toward rebuilding this beautiful city. People from other towns have descended on our devastated neighborhoods to pass out water, popsicles, and bagged lunches to volunteers working tirelessly in near 90 degree heat to clear out flooded homes. It's an incredible thing.

Although the home of the Grand Old Opry was hard hit by the flooding, last night and tonight the legendary Opry went on as planned, albeit in a temporary location. Tonight the symphony filled the open air with the beautiful sound of music in a free performance downtown. Broadway, with all of it's Honkey Tonks, is coming back to life. Tomorrow the annual Steeplechase will go on as scheduled. All of these things giving the people of Nashville necessary moments of normalcy and enjoyment. And further solidifies the idea that while Nashville might be down, she is, by no means, going to be kept down for long.

During the worst moments this past weekend and earlier this week I felt isolated and afraid. I felt for the first time that I never should have left Los Angeles and the safety of my friends and all that unceasing sunshine, after all, this southern California girl knows nothing of flooded basements! But as I watched the days go by and the situation evolve, I began to realize that maybe I'm supposed to be here, that there was much to learn here. Much I *need* to learn here...

Yes, I think I am exactly where I am supposed to be. Right here in this determined, resilient town. And I am grateful that I now call this town *my town.*

Life ain't always beautiful, but it's one hell of a ride...

46

TELL IT LIKE IT IS
(SAY WHAT YOU MEAN, MEAN WHAT YOU SAY)
{ June 9, 2010 }

"The difference between the right word and almost the right word,
is the difference between lightning and a lightning bug".
~ Mark Twain.

The responsibility of being understood lies on the shoulders of the one who is attempting to communicate the message. Choose your words wisely, otherwise, do not be disappointed when the person who is on the receiving end of your communication fails to understand your message.

Conversely, no one has the ability to understand something that you refuse to communicate. People are not mind readers; if you want someone to understand you, open your mouth and let them know what you want them to know...

47

TIME, TIME, TIME...
{ October 12, 2010 }

Who would have thought that I would learn something valuable by watching my 5 year old surf the internet?

Yesterday morning while observing her playing a game on a kids' web site, I noticed how she handled the "download time" by enthusiastically counting down with the timer on the screen. It was as if the waiting was just as much a part of the fun as the actual game that she was waiting on.

She danced in her seat and yelled out in her happy, high-pitched little voice: "13... 12... 11... 10.......".

Which got me thinking about how we react when we (you know, us grown ups) have to wait for things in our lives.

I can honestly say that you are highly unlikely to catch me counting down enthusiastically while I wait for something to download, you know, actually utilizing the time in a positive way, making something good, or fun, out of something, well, at best *annoying*. I'm more likely to be found tapping my fingers (or a foot) in frustration at having been forced to wait (I mean, this is the digital age, right? Can't someone do *something* about all this unnecessary waiting??)

Life ain't always beautiful, but it's one hell of a ride...

Think about it: Have we been so programmed toward "convenience" that having to wait - even mere seconds - becomes a really negative event? If waiting for a few seconds for a download - or someone to pull out of a parking space/get out of their car/merge on to the freeway/pay for their groceries - where does that leave us in dealing with things that take much longer - say, weeks, months or even years?

I know I have (more than once) simply skipped (or at least *attempted* to skip) that which I am forced to wait for if I feel something is taking too long to happen. I've done this at times without even fully knowing *what it is* I might be passing by in my impatience. Perhaps I might be skipping past some interesting knowledge, or perhaps the joy of a simple smile... a great laugh... an opportunity to grow... a valuable life lesson... Maybe even a great personal connection - all of which are positives. Instead, I give in to the negative energy of my impatience and move on believing that much easier, much faster gratification awaits just around the corner. It's just sitting there. Waiting for me.

Much more importantly, consider the time our hearts require to heal from loss or major, perhaps unwanted or unexpected, change. Working within the old adage "time heals all wounds", we shuffle ourselves into a sort of proverbial "waiting room". And while time is a very important component in healing, an often overlooked fact is this: *how you choose to spend that time is as important as the time itself.* Will you spend the time taking in positive activity - self-healing, soothing activities, or helping and positively impacting others (which often translates into a healing activity for oneself), will you seek the lessons to be found in your loss - looking at your loss, as utterly painful as it is, as something to learn and potentially grow from, or perhaps, will you seek out positive inspiration from others, to connect with those who have hurt similarly? Or, rather, will you give away your energy to more negative thoughts/ideas/activities, languishing away, angrily, in that really *really* uncomfortable waiting room chair?

That which has energy, has life.

That which you give your energy to is more likely to manifest in *your* life.

So, as of today I will take the lead of my 5 year old. As time inevitably ticks along during my healing journey, I will look for ways to actively do something good with the time my heart needs to heal. I will put my energy in to the positive in the hopes that I will reap positive rewards and perhaps even have a positive impact on myself and those around me.

Life ain't always beautiful, but it's one hell of a ride...

GO

YEAR 5

{ or: the year I traded my bucket of pain for a spoonful of wisdom }

There are some things we experience that completely alter not only the course of our life, but they alter our very person at a molecular level. This alteration, this change, is not a temporary one. Some experiences or events can cause you to altogether transform into a completely new you. Loss, it seems, particularly the untimely death of one's life partner, is one of those completely life molecule altering events.

There comes a point in many widows' healing journey where we wish that life would "just get back to normal". We're over the chaos, we're tired of change, we are sick of the rollercoaster ride of uncertainty, of feeling bad, and not being able to think straight. We have learned that funny stuff can still be funny even though someone has died, that life doesn't necessarily revolve around the fact that we suffered a deep and tragic loss. We come to realize that we are still human, with normal human feelings, desires, and (ahem) *needs*. To get to this point in the journey is fantastic. When you come to this place, you've likely spent months, maybe even years struggling to find daylight. And now, there it is, and it's glorious! But then you make another discovery that brings a tidal wave of confusion crashing right down on your beautiful, sunshiny moment.

Stopping for a minute to really look over the landscape, you realize that something is… well, strange. Focusing more intently you notice that the landscape you were once so familiar with looks very different – the trees are a different shade of green, the sounds, well, some are much more clear than they used to be, while other sounds are barely audible. As you continue walking along, taking in this odd scene, you pass a mirror, and that's when you realize that it's not the landscape that has changed while you were on your journey, *it's you*.

Life ain't always beautiful, but it's one hell of a ride…

You may hardly recognize that person in the mirror. You may have been walking so long that you never bothered to stop and witness the changes that have been taking place all along, and now, there they all are, *all at once*, staring right back at you in that mirror…

Every step that I had taken in the 4-and-some-odd-years up to this point, was bringing me perfectly in line with this new me that was developing throughout the course of my journey. The 5th year following Ethan's death would be the year that I put my most intense focus on rebuilding my life. And while this was a wonderful turn of emotional events, it also raised a lot of new questions that I hadn't really thought about in previous years. The biggest questions that I had to ask myself were:

Who am I now, because I am definitely not the same girl I was before February 18, 2007, and

What does this new me really (really) want in this new, unfamiliar life?

I think that part of where (and why) we get stuck regarding these questions, is that we have difficulty embracing the idea that we are no longer the same person we were prior to our loss. We spend valuable time fighting this fact, wishing ourselves, and everyone and everything in our lives, back to how it all used to be, back to normal, back to the good 'ol days. This is simply not possible, but it may take a bit of time for some of us to truly accept this. This disruption to our "normal" is compounded by the fact that if we are no longer the same person we used to be, then it's likely we may no longer want the same things for - or in - our lives that we did prior to our loss, either. This realization can be liberating… or it can be debilitating and confusing. If you're anything like me, you may find that it becomes a weird paradox – an absurd combination of both.

When we are grasping so tightly to any little iota of "normalcy", having to deal with the fact that you have changed and your friends haven't; or your priorities have shifted and your chosen career no longer falls in line with those priorities or newly embraced ideals, etc., can all fill us with a sense of dread. Why? Because we know we can't remain stagnant, or frozen in a place we no longer fit, or where we no longer desire to be just because it's comfortable. But that comfort is the very thing we cling so strongly to – it's the thing we can count on to comfort us as we travel what is often a very bumpy road. That dread – fear – triggers our natural fight or flight response. After months or even years of unrelenting emotional ups and downs, and numerous adjustments to change (that whether or not it was unexpected, was most likely unwanted), feeling worn out as we reach this late portion of the journey, we are most tempted to flee from these difficult questions. It's just too much. We're just too… tired.

More change. No. Nope. Not doin' it.

It's easy just to say forget it, I'll just be whatever I am, whatever everyone else is used to me being because I am just too exhausted to struggle through trying to figure out who I am supposed to be in this new life, and definitely way too tired to try to help everyone else around me adjust to this… new stranger.

Yes, it's easiest just to flee from the truth than to fight for it.

But like Elvis once said, "the truth is like the sun. You can shut it out for a while, but it ain't goin' away." And the fact that you are now a new and different "you" than the "you" you used to be isn't going to go away, either, no matter how much you try to resist the idea.

As I focused on rebuilding my life after losing my husband, I made more than my fair share of missteps (there are no mistakes, only lessons).

Life ain't always beautiful, but it's one hell of a ride…

One of those missteps was my attempts at shaking myself lose from my "widowed" status, I had the feeling that in order to move forward in my healing, I somehow had to let go of my loss. I was afraid that others saw it as some kind of crutch. I also felt at times that I didn't want the general image or commonly held idea of what it meant to be a widow to define *me*. And there were times (and I am a bit ashamed of this) that I was concerned about whether or not it was a bit off-putting to potential suitors. And I had enough problems in that particular department without any added help *thank you very much.*

Truth of the matter is, *I am* a widow. Screw what inexperienced, uneducated, or dare I say, ignorant people think of the title. Contrary to popular ideology, that title doesn't say, "little old lady who is sad and alone, who enjoys bingo. Her most exciting social activity is playing with her grandkids." Or, "this chick has a massive shrine to her dead husband, you're always going to be second, dude, run!"

No, what that title "widow" *actually* says is: "I've been to hell and back, and I'm still standing. I'm kind of a bad ass." Which is a totally *true story…*

Being widowed is not what I am – it is not changeable like a career, or hobby – it is a part of *who I am* that is very deeply imbedded within me. My perspective, choices, actions, and ideals are all colored and shaped by this aspect of my new self, and the events and experiences that contributed to creating her. And I am not ashamed of that. Any potential partner who is put off by that is probably not an appropriate partner for someone who has been widowed. Life is hard enough without bringing someone into your life who makes you feel bad about being who you are. And if you're reading this after losing your love, your life has been difficult enough without feeling you have to stop being who you are for yourself (after working so hard to figure out who *yourself* actually is), in order to be a certain something for someone else. Don't go down that road, it's a dead end…

Attempting to put the pieces of yourself and your life back together after they've been blown to little tiny bits is a very tough challenge, made tougher if you have the expectation that what you are putting together looks just like that picture on the box. When we are able to understand and embrace the fact that what you are creating now is not a perfect replica of your past, but, rather, a gorgeous (if not a bit abstract) ever evolving mosaic, in which you lovingly include some of those pieces from the past, yes, but also one that beautifully features an ever growing collection of new pieces from the present, you will find that those earlier questions -

"Who am I now?" And

"What does this new me want in this new life?"

…Just might be answered as your new mosaic begins to take shape and a clear picture develops right before your eyes…

48

THINGS CHANGE,
YET THEY STAY THE SAME...
{ February 18, 2012 }

"Gone - flitted away.
Taken the stars from the night and the sun from the day!
Gone, and a cloud in my heart."
~ Alfred, Lord Tennyson

Ethan, today, as I recognize the 5th anniversary of your death, as always, you are missed with every fiber of my being.

Even after so many years have passed, I continue to seek that peaceful place here on earth, somewhere I might rest my battered heart. I teeter dangerously upon the thin, dilapidated fence separating the stillness from the chaos, the horrible - yet familiar - pain of the past and the frightening uncertainty of the future.

You were my calm before a very dark and most perfect storm. Years alone in a sea of change have left me discombobulated, terrified of each and every passing cloud. Yet for that I have become wiser. I have finely honed survival skills that I could not have attained any other way. I have learned to embrace the small things of beauty, little moments of joy. Those are the things that matter. For the wise know to take the small things of beauty and little moments of joy and knit them together. In time, you'll have something wonderful to wrap yourself up in when the weather turns cold. It may even be big enough to share with those who stood around waiting for the big explosion of happiness to come while letting those small and seemingly insignificant moments pass right under their noses. Ah, yes... Those storm clouds have silver linings...

Now that I am once again safe upon friendly shores I'm trying to get it together. How can something that unraveled so quickly take so very long to untangle and put back together again? And you know what? It doesn't matter which way I put it all back together, I can't make it look like it once did. I've tried so many times that I've lost count. And therein lies one of the most important lessons. I've stopped expecting it to look or feel or be the same. It is impossible. But I *think* it can be good. I sure hope that I am right...

As I carry on with my life here - for however long I might be granted the privilege - know that you are always with me. I may not carry you on my sleeve as I did throughout the earlier years, rather, I've learned to comfortably carry you in my heart, deeply embedded in the softest places of my soul - which is where the most beautiful and cherished memories belong.

My love for you is endless, and my hope is that you are in a wonderfully peaceful place....

Life ain't always beautiful, but it's one hell of a ride...

49

HELLO, IT'S ME
{ June 18, 2012 }

I haven't seen you in a long... long... time.

I know that it's been absolutely ages since I last posted anything [.....]. In all honesty, I've come here many times to write, but every post I created has ultimately been left to languish in the *drafts* folder. However, I've now decided the time has come to dust this off. Why? Well... You see, I have a confession to make: the reasons why I stopped posting [.....] had just as much, if not more, to do with how *I feared other people might perceive me,* than how I truly perceived myself.

I'll explain...

As I've been boppin' on down my little journey through grief over these past 5 years, I have had a few epiphanies. One of those led me to the fact that I was ready for my next adventure, which was [.....]. Another was that I was ready to entertain the idea of dating/relationships. Yes, there were (lots of) others, but I'm going to try to stay focused here.

When I started R.I.S.E. I was, I felt, essentially taking a step away from widowhood, and I felt to continue to write here *and* write there was, well, a bit contradictory. However, I've come to realize over time, that this is totally not the case. Yes, I was wrong (wow, I just put that in writing!). Being a widow is something that is now woven into the very fabric of my being, and no matter where I go, or what I do, widowhood will forever simply be a part of me. To focus on living a wonderful, fulfilled life in spite of my loss, and helping others toward doing the same, doesn't mean I have to be perfect. News flash, Stephanie: *no one is.* In fact, quite contrary to my initial thoughts, perhaps this admission – this show of imperfection – is the very thing that may serve to help people most – which is where my passion lies...

That leads me to the *other* thing: relationships. There was this feeling that I had, that made me think that by continuing to expose my emotional, widowed self publicly, I would be sending the wrong signal(s) to any potential suitor. Not that I'm enjoying a *flood* of offers (chortle) my dating life resembles something more like a small splash in the occasional shallow (and quickly evaporating) puddle left over from a brief rain shower on a 100 degree day. But *I digress*...

I just kind of had it in my head that to move forward with my "single" life meant I needed to completely let go of my "widowed" life, or at least, my publicly seen/read widowed life. But as before, there's that whole fabric thing again. It's simply who and what I am now. I can date 100 men (hellooooo!) and I would still be a widow. My life, overall, would still be colored by my experiences stemming from, and associated with, my loss. I guess it's just taken me a minute to figure that out. It's also taken me a minute to choose myself first – meaning any said *potential suitors* would just have to deal with the fact that **a)** I am a widow, **b)** I will always be a widow, **c)** my life will continue to be marked in certain ways by my experience – likely forever, and **d)** I write about it.

So there.

I'm not sure, at this point, exactly how much I am going to be writing here. I would guess it will be as often as the occasion, or need, arises for me to do so. I'm just going to go with the flow.

It feels good to be back. It feels good to be myself...

50

NEVER LET ME SLIP, 'CAUSE IF I SLIP, THEN I'M SLIPPIN'
{ July 11, 2012 }

There was a time, not long ago when I would have been considered by many (probably most) to be a "hard worker". There was nothing I wouldn't do for the company or our clients.

Work in the middle of the night? Sure.

On weekends? No problem.

There was no such thing as a holiday from my job. Heck, my husband and I never even took a honeymoon, lest we'd fail to be there if any of our clients needed us. To put in 10/12/14 hours was not terribly unusual for either of us (especially him). It was nothing to really complain about, it's just what it was.

It was partially to do with the sheer demands of our chosen professions, and partially due to the demands we chose, individually, to put upon ourselves. Knowing that if we weren't around to do it, someone else most certainly *was*. Fail to be ready and waiting one too many times, and find yourself out on your ear. Both of us were a little too ambitious, and maybe even a little too proud, to allow *that* to happen.

When Ethan died, understandably, I absolutely fell apart. For the first time in 10 years work was the furthest thing from my mind. I was unable to get out of bed for weeks, and unable to concentrate on anything for more than two-and-a-half minutes for months. I was useless as an employee, and I was blessed to have an employer who was more than just an employer, he was more than my friend - we considered each other *family*, and thus, I was very generously allowed a lot of time and space to grieve, for which I will forever be grateful. Eventually I would have to return to work, or bow out and allow someone else to be hired to do the job I was still being paid to do. This was completely understandable; of course, there was a business to be run. Quite frankly, by the time my boss delicately presented my options to me (come back or bow out), it was probably time for me to return to work, if for no other reason than I really needed a distraction. It was time to do something else other than sit around and wallow in my grief. However, the employee he got upon my return was not the same girl as she was prior to February 18, 2007.

When I finally went back to work I was sad, angry, listless, unable to concentrate, often disinterested, and very distracted - not only by the grief, but also by the criminal trial that was still ongoing for the person who killed Ethan - which, because of extensions, continuances and other nonsense, would drag on for the better part of a year. Unfortunately, however, now that I have come 5 1/2 years down the road, I'm beginning to believe that my ability to really "stay on the grind", as my peers would say, has seemingly disappeared permanently.

A little over three years ago the small (but very fruitful) organization I worked for was forced to do some restructuring. I probably would have been able to stay, however, I knew it would have meant a significant reduction in salary, so I used this excuse to take the option of the permanent layoff. As much as I looked upon my employer and those I worked with as my family, I can't begin to tell you how *relieved* I was by the fact that I could finally stop and regroup. Take a minute to find my mojo.

We all know that it's much easier to find something while you look for it in a slow, methodical manner, than it is while you're attempting to hurry out the out the door, late for work (which I was daily). I don't see why my "mojo" would be any different than my glasses or house keys.

Every day that I went to work in the state I was in I felt like a complete failure - to myself, my boss, everyone I worked with and for. I was simply a shell of my old self - there was just nothing going on on the inside. The love I had for the demands of my job, the joy I felt at finishing a project, or making something great happen, or a successful event - all... just... gone... I knew it, and I'm fairly certain everyone else felt it, too.

Of course, no one ever complained. If I was offered any advice, it always came from a place of love, never disappointment in my work. I know that it was just impossible for anyone to see that no matter how much I would love to have been able to take their advice, it just wasn't that simple.

You see, I just wasn't ready. My heart wasn't ready. Or, at least that's what I thought then. I always thought that at some point that excitement I had for work, that thrill of the job well done, my professional pride, would someday return on its own.

However, now I'm beginning to think that some things, once gone, can't be reclaimed.

After leaving my former job, I moved to Nashville - you know, *to get myself back together.* Since moving here 3 years ago, there are a million ways in which I've healed, grown, and evolved. But one area in which I don't seem to have experienced much recovery is my ability to concentrate on work, or much of anything, really, for more than 5 minutes. This has been boggling me for quite a while, because I'm not sure why I am unable to reclaim this part of myself that was once my strongest attribute.

I've tried doing the old stuff... Nothin'

I've tried doing some new stuff... Still, nothin'

I'm currently in the midst of a year long course that I've been wanting to do for a couple of years, and while I'm in class I'm really excited about it, yet, I can't seem to focus on homework, or the extra work that I need to really get the most out of it. I've gone from being a complete "self starter" to a virtual "non-starter". And I'm scared.

I'm scared that after all of this time, if I haven't managed to regain my career-girl mojo, that drive to get it done, that thrill of the completed project/task, the putting in the extra effort to do it bigger and better simply because *that's how I roll*, that it's possible I may not ever taste the sweetness of any of it again. Would I even recognize it if I did taste it? Has it been so long since I had it, would I just want to spit it out if I *did* get a spoonful - like developing an aversion to cake after giving up sugar for 3 years?

Have I permanently "slipped"? And is the slope too slippery to climb back up? Has my professional drive turned into the proverbial greased pig?

I try to be gentle with myself as much as possible. But I'm seriously at a complete loss for what to do about this, so I've reached for the tough (self) love. For the first time in 5 1/2 years, I'm willing to admit that maybe I've *fallen off* (shutters). If you know me, you know that's like a boxer walking into the middle of the ring during a heavyweight bout and just laying down. And much like most boxers, I'd rather take my chances over nine rounds with someone twice my size than admit fa-.

Fail-.

Failu-

See... I can't even say the word...

But, even with the shocking admission (even if it's only partial), the question still remains: how do I get as ambitious again on the inside, as I've always seemed to remain on the outside? I've been staring at this wall for a while now, and I just can't seem to figure out how to "get over it"...

51

AND MAYBE SOMEDAY WE WILL FIND THAT IT REALLY WASN'T WASTED TIME
{ July 17, 2012 }

So this is really one for the wids...

Over the past five years, I've undergone many, many changes. Most of them good (discovering purpose, setting better priorities), some of them not so good (I'm definitely "fluffier" - although that probably has more to do with a combination of age and lethargy, than some sort of aftereffect of my loss...). And then there are those things that at first glance I thought were "good", but upon further examination, may not necessarily be so.

Lately I've been really contemplating relationships. Not because I'm in one (my romantic relationship drought is a subject for an entirely different post), but I have been on a few dates over the past few years and I have come to realize that the way that I approach, and deal with relationships (even potential ones) is COMPLETELY different now than it was before my loss.

From what I understand this isn't terribly unusual.

As widows, we have a great understanding of what it feels like to lose the one you love with a finality that you don't experience under any other circumstance. In the midst of a love going right, it all... just... ends... The lesson that this often leaves us with is to appreciate and respect love, and a loving partner, because we realize that neither are necessarily a right, but, rather, an incredible *privilege*. And that privilege can absolutely be taken away. Abruptly, and without warning.

We might find that we want to spend a lot less time, well, *wasting* time. This might mean only focusing on the positives in our partner, deciding to choose being "happy" over being "right", or, for some people, making quick decisions about relationships. And here is where it gets personal for me.

I do find myself making quick decisions about relationships, or potential relationships, and that can be a good thing - I don't waste time with anyone with whom I do not see a future. I also don't waste time on senseless nonsense, games, etc. Those are good things, right? Well, I think I may have discovered that there might also be a downside to this *speed reading...*

Since I'm so quick to make decisions, could I possibly be making decisions *too fast*? I realize that some things (and people!) take time to reveal themselves, and in my desire to "not waste time", am I making premature determinations about a person's, or a relationship's potential?

You see, it's kind of like I'm playing with a stacked deck. *I* realize there is not time to waste because of my experience. However, if the person across from me, who hasn't had a similar experience to me, is still doing things "the old way", does that make their way *the wrong way*? To them, there may be all the time in the world. They may not suss up a relationship in the same manner, or speed, in which I do, because they do not understand the urgency.

So, let's just imagine there was someone who was interested in me, but perhaps they had a more laid back approach - no urgency, no big hurry. And I take that "no hurry" to mean "no interest"? If I think there is "no interest", I'm naturally going to see there being "no future". And this is the point where I turn to my legendary aloofness (again, deserving of it's own separate post...), pretty much driving the train to its sudden, but quite absolute *dead end*...

But what if I've got it all wrong?

Could my *hair trigger*, my desire to not waste time ultimately cause me to *waste a good potential opportunity*? How do I revert back to doing things "the old way", when I've been so (traumatically) enlightened? Can I possibly ignore my hard-won knowledge, and act with utter ignorance of the lessons?

52

I'M OUT ON A LIMB
{ July 21, 2012 }

Like many people who have undergone a life-altering loss, I've spent a lot of time over the past few years trying to "find myself". When your existence is shattered in such a way that you no longer recognize any part of yourself, or the world in which you lived, this can be a long and daunting process. It's almost as if you don't even have a recognizable starting point.

In terms of what to do with my life, I've pondered many things. Since I spent over a decade working in music and entertainment, that's always been at the forefront of my thoughts. I did continue to work in the business for a couple of years after E's death, and, yes, it was profitable and satisfying... to a point. There was something about the business that just wasn't as wholly fulfilling as I needed my life path to be. I had changed so much, and the entertainment industry, as anyone who works in it knows, is a very selfish business. I'm not complaining, it simply is what it is. I knew I wanted - no, needed - to focus my energy and attention in a more selfless way, and I really needed to spend more of my time and attention on my children. Two things that are not easy in a 24/7, highly ego driven industry.

About a year after moving to Nashville I obtained my certification as a Grief Recovery Specialist. That was an accomplishment I am very proud of. And a program I do believe in - for a very specific group of people. It is not for everyone, and I also felt that while helping people through that very difficult process was and is amazing, I also really wanted to focus on living a positive life after loss. Not to focus solely on grief or death, but to focus on recreation of LIFE - because those of us who are going through it are *going through it* because we are still here. We have to figure out not only how to continue to *live*, but we need to figure out how to live a positive, purposeful, fulfilling life, when the life we wanted - the life we had - ceases to exist.

I'd learned so much, and grown so much through my experience, I wanted to figure out a way to pass along the lessons; someway to help others create a pathway to their own growth.

So I decided a couple of years ago that in addition to my Grief Recovery certification, that I wanted to become a Certified Professional Coach, or, as I like to call myself, a *Positive Change Strategist*. I sat on the decision for a while because I knew that it would take a lot of money and a lot of time to go through the process of certification - certification that isn't actually necessary to practice as a coach, however, I'm not one to do things halfway (unless, perhaps, we're talking about the laundry, my half-way-ness clearly demonstrated by the ever growing clean pile sitting on top of the dryer). I knew that I really wanted to learn as much as I could about various methods in a thorough manner, and get many, many hours of practice, because, I believe, the better my education, the more rigorously I train, the greater benefit I am to the greatest number of people.

So this year I finally embarked on a year long course of study. And as I immersed myself in my studies, I felt so at peace! I began to truly believe that this was EXACTLY where I was supposed to be.

Life ain't always beautiful, but it's one hell of a ride...

As part of our learning, we spend a lot of time coaching our classmates. Eventually, however, you are required to take a step out and start coaching real clients. Uh oh. Yeah, this is where my happy little jog ran into some 5 foot high personal hurdles...

It was at this point along the journey on my new path, my peace gave way to absolute and utter terror.

Paralyzed by fear, I was suddenly beginning to doubt myself, and this crazy decision I had made. I mean, who was I that I thought I could coach people toward a better life? Who would want to seek my guidance or assistance?? I was honestly ready to throw in the towel, rather than have to face judgment for this new path that I had chosen.

Judgment by my former peers, who would quickly toss me out of the *cool kids club* that I was no longer eligible to be a member of, because I'd chosen a new path.

Judgment by those in the widowed community who might think I was arrogant by believing I could help people regarding a journey that we had *all* been through. What could I possibly know that they didn't already, and how could I have the nerve to charge for whatever it was I thought I knew??

Judgment by those who might somehow look at me as profiting from the death of my husband, since this new path revealed itself as I worked my way through my loss.

Judgment by the entire world (I know, I'm soooo drama) that I wasn't good enough, smart enough, capable enough - anything enough, really - to be taken seriously as a coach, let alone viewed as a *good* coach...

I spent many days and nights thinking about this. About being judged. And why I was even worried about being judged. And it really all came back to my own fear of failure - failing myself, failing my family's expectations, and failing those who might come to me as clients. I knew that coaching would require me to help many people through their own fears regarding failure. How could I help others in an area where I couldn't seem to help myself? I have no doubt about where my heart, my passion lies, but was I really up to the challenges that this new path might present?

What I determined after much thought, is that we judge ourselves *far* more than anyone else might judge us. Sure, some of our friends, family members, or peers might be little judgey-judgers, but in reality, very few of them actually are. At the end of the day, the biggest judgey-judgers of us *are ourselves*.

So I decided to stop judging myself, and move forward with this path that I am so excited, so very passionate about. I managed to muster up the courage to go out seeking clients, which I found - quickly, in fact. And while I'm still working my way through some of my fears, I've come to realize that the anticipation of going out on a limb was far scarier than the actual being out on the limb. I've encountered no judgment from anyone outside of myself, and the feedback I'm getting is all very positive and constructive. And while, sure, it's a little uncomfortable hanging all alone out here, I know that we all have to get outside of our comfort zone if we really hope to grow.

Yes, I AM exactly where I'm supposed to be.

So, now I've tasted a little bit of the fruit that hangs so provocatively out at the end of the limb, and it's pretty sweet! I think I'll stay out here for a little while and fill up my basket with the good stuff. And when I'm done, there's another branch I'm eyeballing. Now that I know that it ain't so bad after all, I can't wait to scamper up there and gather up all of the deliciousness.

This time no waiting, no heavy anticipation, no false fears... Just action.

Life ain't always beautiful, but it's one hell of a ride...

53

YOU AND TEQUILA
{ August 14, 2012 }

I don't always drink tequila, but when I do...

If you happen to read my other blog, you may have seen yesterday's post about being honest with yourself. In that post I mention a few "Universal Truths" that we all should recognize and accept in order to step toward greater freedom in our lives. One of those "Universal Truths" was this:

Universal Truth #4: You always have a choice.

A year ago, I may not have included this truth. Because of all I had experienced in my life, I couldn't accept the idea that we always have a choice. All of the things that had happened to me, the road I believed I was forced to travel because of the bad decisions of other people, or because of my familial or personal responsibilities, seemed to be a really good, legitimate argument against this... *truth*... But one day I learned that my reasons for not accepting this were simply nothing more than a foundation for my excuses to make certain safe or comfortable choices, or to avoid change.

And I had this light bulb moment - or, rather, this lesson was handed to me (you may even say it was *served* in the classic b-boy sense of the word) - one night in a downtown tequila bar, no less.

I don't really talk much about my personal relationships for the sake of the privacy of the person on the other side of the respective relationship, but mostly because, well, there really aren't many to speak of. However, maybe too many lonely Friday and Saturday nights watching Sex And The City re-runs has me tapping into my inner Carrie Bradshaw (yeah right... if only I had so much to talk about psssshhhh)...

Anywayz...

So there I was, out enjoying a great LA evening, with a good looking guy, having a great time, when someone thought going to a tequila bar was a good idea. And it was... at least for a little while.

The drinks were good, the atmosphere was fun, but in the midst of all of that frivolity, a conversation about my living situation commenced. Now, I can't recount word-for-word how the conversation went exactly, there was, after all, tequila involved. So I'll do some (loose) paraphrasing here...

It's important to note at this point that I've been living in Nashville for 3 1/2 years and I had come to the conclusion some time ago that it wasn't working out for me, and I was terribly unhappy. Out of fear of how this revelation would affect (hurt) others, I was reluctant to tell anyone, and instead existed in a very unhappy state. But that story in greater detail is subject for another post. Back to *this* story...

I was ~~arguing~~ debating the point that regardless of the fact that I wasn't happy where I was, I couldn't just pack up and move because of this, that, and a third.

Tequila Guy: It's always your choice. You can do whatever you want.

Me: I can't just do whatever I want. I'm worried that if I do *this*, the consequences will be x, y, and z. And I'm afraid if I do *that*, so and so will be

Life ain't always beautiful, but it's one hell of a ride...

hurt! I can't just go around making people feel like that, I have a responsibility...

Tequila Guy: Yes, okay, there are always consequences to the choices we make, but you still always have a choice.

The light bulb in my head began to glow, albeit ever so slightly.

And, really, I knew at that moment that should have been the end of the conversation. But I have a bit of a history with Tequila Guy, and something about him makes me want to out wit and out smart him, though I rarely ever do. Friendly competition? Power play? I don't know, but suffice it to say I wasn't giving up the win that easy. Trouble is, my hardheadedness (read: temper) mixed with a little (*cough*) mezcal meant my point was pretty much dead in the water - floating along in a life raft ignoring that distinct whistle - that sound of the air leaking out. I fought on...

Me: That's SO not true! Other people do things that affect our lives in ways that we don't have a choice in (of course, a nod to the person who killed Ethan).

(HA! Take THAT!)

Tequila Guy: Yes, we can't control everything or everyone else, but we always have a choice when it comes to our own actions and decisions (again, I'm paraphrasing, but this is the gist of his rebuttal).

And so we continued back and forth, but as I quickly ran out of legitimate points to support my original position, and I began to actually understand what he was saying, I began to get angry. Tequila Guy was cool as a cucumber, which, he usually always is, and which, of course, made me even angrier (which it always did)…

All the years I had been able to put my decisions, my choices on the shoulders of someone or something else. My safety net was being consumed by the tide faster than they could line up shots on the bar. All the times I hid from personal responsibility by convincing myself I had to do a certain something, make a particular choice, because, well I had no choice! And now, in a downtown tequila bar, through the haze of a couple "sueñas", it was all suddenly... so... clear... I was fighting my own truth.

I was reluctant - no, no... flat out unwilling - to accept this change to my story (you know, the part where I have to take full responsibility), so I just got mad instead. My baseless ~~argument~~ point had finally deflated until there was nothing left to keep it afloat.

Tequila guy just stood there, with a smirk on his face.

But it wasn't the selfish, chilly smirk that says I won. Rather, it was the knowing smirk of someone who knew they'd just managed to teach the girl-who-knew-everything a lesson. And not just any 'ole lesson. A ginormo, life changing one.

A-hole.

Fresh out of white flags, instead I capped off my performance with an improvised stomp-and-pout. By the next morning I had recovered, my only noticeable injuries being my bruised ego. I left LA that morning and returned to Nashville with an awful lot more than I had left with.

This whole episode happened nearly a year ago now, and I have since had time to come to understand, accept, and apply this very important lesson. There are key moments in our lives when we are truly expanded into new realms. Truly evolutionary moments. I had experienced, earned, lost, learned SO much since Ethan passed away, and one of those things I had learned - that I talk to others about every day - was the fact that our own choices are responsible for shaping our happiness. Yet, I hadn't crossed the line into truly and absolutely taking total responsibility for my OWN choices -

Life ain't always beautiful, but it's one hell of a ride...

including those I had made in the past. Because of that lack of ownership, I could never live in complete truth. Who would have thought I would have taken all of that away from a night in a tequila bar. But life is strange that way...

Life ain't always beautiful, but it's one hell of a ride...

54

GOT TO KEEP MY IRONS IN THE FIRE
{ August 21, 2012 }

But how many irons is *too many* irons? And why I can't I seem to figure out how to prioritize it all?

I discovered a long time ago that if I wanted anything done well (read: right), it's best to just do it myself. Trouble is, being a one (wo)man band is more difficult than that guy on the Venice boardwalk makes it look.

I have this tendency to come up with a thousand ideas and the desire to implement them all - without delegating any of it to anyone else. Okay, in all honesty, my current issue with delegation is as much to do with finances as it is to do with my control issues, but in addition to both of those, I have the need to prove to myself that I can learn it and do it, which can be a bit of a dangerous game if one is not careful.

Yes, if one is not careful, one may find herself throwing it all up in the air - and catching none of it. All you end up learning is that you can't do everything.

Sigh

Right now I'm in between classes and I have decided to utilize the next four weeks before the next classes begin, doing a self-study course and working on a new website design [.....], which will require I learn a few additional skills. On top of that I'm working with coaching clients, creating new

Life ain't always beautiful, but it's one hell of a ride...

coaching programs and developing workshops I am planning for the end of the fourth quarter. Oh yeah, and I'm going to go and move my kid into college, feed, do homework and hang out with the 7 year old (who also wants to do swimming and Girl Scouts!), find some time to read a book or two that I've been meaning to get to, and get this house together so I can get it on the market, because on top of all of that... I want to move.

Whew!

I know it's really not that much stuff, my trouble really comes in the prioritizing of it all. And regarding that very issue, I am thus far failing miserably.

I've written about my career-girl skills slipping away in a previous post, and I think that is what is most frustrating about this whole thing. The old me would have been juggling all these things and thriving in the chaos. And while I'm excited about regaining a sense of drive that I've truly missed, I'm not sure how to find the middle - that space between "doing nothing" and "doing EVERYTHING". There's got to be a place where I can feel a sense of accomplishment, achieve some of my most important goals, have the quality time I wish to give to my children, and get the day to day stuff done (writing/coursework/reading/etc.) without feeling like I'm going crazy. I never could prioritize well before, and that always made my life, and our family life, a bit chaotic.

After everything I have been through in the past 5 1/2 years, I've had enough chaos for an entire lifetime, thank you very much. I also know that my kids were always on the losing end of all of that chaos, and I refuse to allow that to continue to be a part of their story. Quite frankly, I no longer want that to be a part of my story. Where the family is concerned, when there is too much chaos, everybody tends to lose.

Life ain't always beautiful, but it's one hell of a ride...

Yes, it seems the new me is averse to chaos... Downright allergic.   I just want stuff to happen peacefully... perfectly... yet completely *my way*. I'm not sure that it's possible. But I'm not sure I can let go of stuff, either. It's quite a conundrum. So I continue to keep all of my irons in the fire, and hope they don't get so hot that I end up getting burned.

It still amazes me that after all of this time I am still adjusting to my situation, my(new)self. You'd think that I'd have all of this figured out by now, yet the journey is constantly full of revelations, and the parts of me that have changed have yet to completely figure out how to play nicely with the parts of me that remain the same...

55

CHECK YO-SELF,
BEFORE YOU WRECK YO-SELF
{ September 18, 2012 }

I'm not really sure what's gotten into me lately, and why I'm suddenly stuck on the topic of relationships. I'm not sure if it's because I wish I *were* in a relationship, or I don't want to be in a relationship (but I'm not sure I want to be stuck with *me* for the rest of my life without at least some sort of buffer). I don't know if it's about my fear of relationships (power, loss, and all kinds of other *things-that-go-bump-in-the-night* nonsense), or because, as history has shown, well, I just really suck at them. Most likely it's some unfortunate, twisted, paradoxical combination of all of those things, with a little "I turned 40 this year and I'm single" sprinkled in for flavor, that has me so fixated on the topic.

So anyway, I was minding my own business on yet another dateless Saturday night, when I ran out of wine. Once I got over the shock and disappointment, I realized that there was nothing left to do really, but sit here...

And think...

And so there I sat... thinkin'... mulling over the current affairs of my (cough) *current affairs*, which led me (eventually) to wonder: How is it we misrepresent ourselves and/or our feelings to the world - and by "the world" I

Life ain't always beautiful, but it's one hell of a ride...

mean *the opposite sex* - and then we get mad because we don't get what we really want?

Follow along with me...

A lot of people who know me would probably describe me as strong. Some might even go one step further and describe me, perhaps, as *tough*. And while these would seem pretty accurate at first glance, one I consider a positive (and true), and one - the latter - not so much. These... descriptions... are nothing new, and certainly didn't begin with E's death. No, they're words that I've been hearing to describe me for a long time now. However, I know that they don't tell the *whole story*...

I guess you could say I'm a case of hard and crunchy on the outside, and all soft in the center. Unfortunately, to get to my center you just might break a tooth first, which may leave you a bit reluctant to take another bite.

I'm not quite sure which point of pressure has caused my outside edges to get so... so... *crunchy*. I do know that I wasn't always this way. Looking back, I can't really tell you when things began to change for me, I just woke up one day and my outside was this... strange person my inside didn't quite recognize.

Whether it was simply my life in general - and trust me, there's not enough time to go into *all-a-that* - or my career of choice, in an industry where weak (wo)men are regularly eaten alive (I've seen it with my own eyes!) - I can't really say. What I do know is that years of having to protect myself (or believing I needed to protect myself) in some form or another, from some *thing* or another, has caused me to develop this crunchy coating, which seems to have gotten thicker through the years. And while it existed long before my loss, it would be fair to say that it was compounded, to perhaps a large extent, by it.

Life ain't always beautiful, but it's one hell of a ride...

But I know that while it may be what many people see, it's not a complete representation of who I am.

It may be shocking to some, but in spite of what my outsides may say, on the inside I really *love* love. Always have. Throughout my life I've wanted more than anything simply *to* love and *be* loved.   And I want what every other girl wants: someone whose eyes light up when they see me, who smiles when they think of me. Who can't wait to be near me. In many ways I am fortunate to be able to say that, while we certainly had our ups and downs, I absolutely experienced those things in my relationship with E.

But, unfortunately circumstances came to pass that have led me, once again, to be alone and, once again, desiring these feelings and experiences.

Also unfortunate, is the fact that on the outside, I'm fierce, fearless... aloof... with a you-can't-phase-me demeanor. You might even think I was a little power hungry if you met me on the ~~right~~ wrong day. No, you would probably never know what was going on in my insides if you only knew my outsides.

My point? Well, I guess my real conundrum lies in the fact that my outsides are man repellent. And when my outsides aren't repelling men, they're sending out some high frequency signal that is attracting all the wrong ones (I was going to use a dog whistle analogy here, but I don't know that it will help my case...). In short: my outsides are *wreckin' my game*.

While men might respect a woman for being strong and independent, I've found as I've gotten older, that this respect is often only held at arms length. In my experience, men may compliment, even admire those attributes in female family members, friends, or associates, they don't necessarily want to *date* someone within whom those particular attributes *floweth over... all over* the dang place. *And* a man will perceive those attributes as being far worse if

Life ain't always beautiful, but it's one hell of a ride...

he feels (correctly, or erroneously) that they are being used *against him* in any way. Further, if that independence translates to aloofness, that definitely compounds the problem. I'm not sure any man really appreciates a woman who acts like she doesn't care about how that man feels about her. And a man who *really doesn't* care about how a woman feels about him, is a) not really into her, and/or b) is most likely a man who doesn't know *how* to feel, and what girl wants to date either one of *those* guys?

Look, you should have known when I said "ran out of wine" that nothing good was going to come of this. Welcome to Stephanie's world, please drive through...

But if it's true that you get what you give, if I'm walking around giving the outward impression that I don't care what anyone thinks of me, or that I don't need anyone, or that I am unaffected by whether someone has feelings for me or not, I'm ultimately going to attract men who don't care, don't/won't have feelings for me, or who *don't think of me at all*. To get anything different, I need to do something different - I must be willing to risk being my *real* self.

This idea of being my *real self* is not so difficult simply because it involves being vulnerable, which, yes, is hard enough. It's difficult because it's going to take an awful lot of time and effort to create a hole big enough in my thick, crunchy outsides to be able to get in and *find her*.

Apparently I'll need some additional tools for this job, like, say, a pick axe and maybe a torch.

So, okay... While I sat there pondering the fact that I'd like to *not* sit at home... alone... *every* Saturday night, and, yes, while it would be nice to have someone in my life who lights up when I walk in the room or smiles when they think of me - oh Hell, who am I kidding? It would just be nice to have someone with enough decency to return a dang phone call - yeah, while that would be nice, and while I'm willing to *check myself* regarding my own contribution to my current... situation... *here's what:* I'm not entirely 100% sure that making myself more emotionally transparent is really going to completely change the game for me.

Why not?

Well, because while I recognize my own shortcomings, and openly admit that I could probably work on them - is that truly the crux of my problem? Or is it something... bigger... and much different than that? Is it even about *me*?

56

HAPPY BIRTHDAY, E
{ 12.12.12 }

Aaron Rodgers Day, a big kick-ass concert in NJ, and the beginning of the end of days - all on your birthday. I can't help but think somehow you've got a hand in all of this. After all, *there are no coincidences*.

Happy Birthday, E. I sure wish you were here to celebrate it with us "in real life", as Ava would say.

Ava and I will be sending you up some balloons later. She's indicated that she would like to send you a special note, so be on the lookout for that...

This evening there will be cupcakes and cheap champagne in your honor (see, honey, I'm still keepin it real). Wherever you are, my love, I hope that you are in excellent company, smiling that great big smile of yours, espousing intriguing, yet utterly useless information, and making the other side a better place.

We miss you today, and every day. xoxo

Life ain't always beautiful, but it's one hell of a ride...

57

COLD AS ICE
{ February 6, 2013 }

"To love at all is to be vulnerable. Love anything, and your heart will certainly be wrung and possibly broken. If you want to make sure of keeping it intact, you must give your heart to no one, not even to an animal. Wrap it carefully round with hobbies and little luxuries; avoid all entanglements; lock it up safe in the casket or coffin of your selfishness. But in that casket- safe, dark, motionless, airless–it will change. It will not be broken; it will become unbreakable, impenetrable, irredeemable." ~ C. S. Lewis

C. S. was definitely on to something with this one.

I think that it's natural for us, when we've been through the loss of our husband or wife, to want to hide our hearts for many reasons. And I think that our experience makes it especially easy for us to choose to hide our hearts in the sand out of the fear of additional heartbreak. The thing is, when we cut ourselves off from the prospect of loving and being loved, while we may think ourselves, perhaps, safe, ultimately each day that goes by in our closed off state, our hearts underutilized – or not utilized at all – for its intended purpose, it begins to forget how to do what it was made to do best.

Much like our muscles, our heart begins to atrophy.

Now I realize clearly that a lot of widows and widowers are simply not ready to wrap their brains around a new relationship. I'm not talking about those folks. I'm talking about the ones who know they are lonely, would like to have a partner in their life, but have declared to the world that they aren't interested in dating or relationships because they don't want to get hurt.

Here's what: love flows in and out of the same channel. If you aren't open to receiving it, you aren't open to giving it. And vice versa. If you want something positive in your life and you purposely deny yourself, that blocked flow will start to overflow into other relationships and aspects of your life.

Dating, and relationships, and love, can be scary, I know. And, no – no one wants to get their heart broken. And I'm not saying that everyone out there needs to go find a boyfriend or a girlfriend. I'm just saying, if you know that you would like to have someone in your life, you know that you want to give love and be loved, don't deny yourself just because you are afraid of being vulnerable. Life is one big vulnerable experience. There is no such thing as perfectly safe existence, unless you are going to move into a hermetically sealed tent and never come out. It is by being vulnerable that we allow ourselves to be open to all of the beauty and bounty this world has to offer, and to me that – in and of itself – is totally worth it.

Even if it means a perfectly fine day gives way to the occasional hail storm.

So don't lock yourself away, because I promise you, you aren't doing yourself as much favor as you think… ♥

EPILOGUE

Back in 2007, when I first began this journey, there was no way in the world I would have believed that I would not only survive the death of my husband, but that I would find myself moving on from a career that I adored and worked hard to succeed in, sell the home that we bought together to raise our family in, and move 2,000 miles away to entirely new city in the hopes of getting a fresh start. The ways in which my life has changed are many – and some of those changes are quite profound, and were completely unexpected.

It is amazing what we can do when we decide that though something awful has occurred, we have not yet reached the end of *our* story.

I put these posts together in chronological order so that you - the reader, who may have found yourself in a world of loss and grief that you never fathomed - could discover a sense of connection to another who has walked a while in similar shoes, but most importantly, you would find in these posts a sense of hope as you read about my personal struggles, epiphanies, resolution, and eventual evolution, in real time, as I experienced it all.

When you lose your husband or wife, or life partner, no matter the stage of life really, but specifically when their passing is untimely, and they (and you), are still quite young, it seems to go against the very order of things. It's not *normal*. But as a wise woman once said: "Normal is an illusion. What is normal to the spider is chaos to the fly". When we lose our spouse, we learn very quickly that life will never be the same as it once was, no matter how hard we wish. In our search for normal we discover a *new normal*.

Life ain't always beautiful, but it's one hell of a ride…

Normal life becomes the life that we choose to create for ourselves as we re-create ourselves. It may contain parts of the old life, but, oh, it's *very* different - simply for the very fact that *we* are now different.

As I was assembling the material for this book, and read back through the posts I've decided to include here, it opened up a flood of old memories about my life with my husband, but more than that, I was able to see clearly all of the cycles I went through on my way to becoming who I am today - 8 years after his untimely and sudden death. The anger in the beginning is palpable. I was drowning in anger throughout the months and years following Ethan's death. It is no more visible than in post #33, where I vow to never forgive the young man who started us all on this long, unbelievable (and unwanted) journey. I don't think it's unusual to feel such deep-seeded anger inside toward someone who has caused such loss, such pain, to so many. In fact, it is the very rare, highly evolved person who wouldn't at least in the beginning feel such anger. But as time wore on, I learned one of the most valuable lessons of all: the anger I had toward him wasn't affecting him in the least. The anger I had toward him was poisoning me, slowly killing me from the inside out. If I ever hoped to find a sense of peace, of balance, I would need to get that poison out of my system.

While I did eventually manage to rid myself of all of that angry poison, and I can say with all honesty I carry no more anger regarding what this young man did, I will also admit that the path to forgiveness was no easy journey. Not in the least. I struggled with the very idea of forgiveness, afraid that forgiving him was somehow excusing him, or no longer holding him responsible. I learned through a lot of soul searching that my ideas regarding forgiveness at the time couldn't have been further from the truth of what it really means to forgive. Forgiveness brings us peace by taking away the power that a person's negative actions, or a negative event has over us. Our bodies are our spiritual and emotional homes. And an angry home can never feel peace or joy, and it can never expand, it will always be in a state of tight contraction. As long as I was angry with him, as long as I stayed angry about what he had caused to happen, I couldn't move beyond that place. I would always remain stuck there, in a tight little angry ball. I would continue to use him, and his actions, and my anger regarding it all as my crutch.

I was angry at everyone and everything - all of the time. I felt so utterly punished by what had happened that I was almost certain that I had done something in another life that was so awful, so *vile,* that I had to continue to pay for it in this life. What I was not able to understand then, which I do now, is that I wasn't being punished. In fact, I was *fortunate* to still be here. To have a life in front of me to live. I could choose to spend the rest of it angry about things I couldn't change, or I could try to resolve my emotional sticky-stuff and find forgiveness and acceptance, so that I could have a chance at living peacefully, and perhaps once again find joy in this life.

If you are reading this after having lost your husband or wife, the final thought I would like to share with you is this: make it your number one priority to try to make peace with where you are, and where you've been. There is no such thing as the perfect grief journey – no direct route to healing and happiness. At some point almost all of us will think we've lost our minds, or react out of negative emotion, make a choice or decision we might wish we hadn't, or attempt an ill-fated short cut attempt (or three). We are all just humans, trying to survive the unimaginable. Forgive yourself and prepare yourself to move forward with your life, because you are still here, and you deserve an abundant and beautiful experience going forward, regardless of what lies in your past. Once you do, your entire world will begin to change.

Life ain't always beautiful, but it's one hell of a ride...

You will begin to see more light, and you will begin to once again find yourself able to embrace the possibility of *possibilities.*

None of us wants to live without our loves, but we can, and you will, I promise you.

www.ingramcontent.com/pod-product-compliance
Lightning Source LLC
Chambersburg PA
CBHW081646270326
41933CB00018B/3365